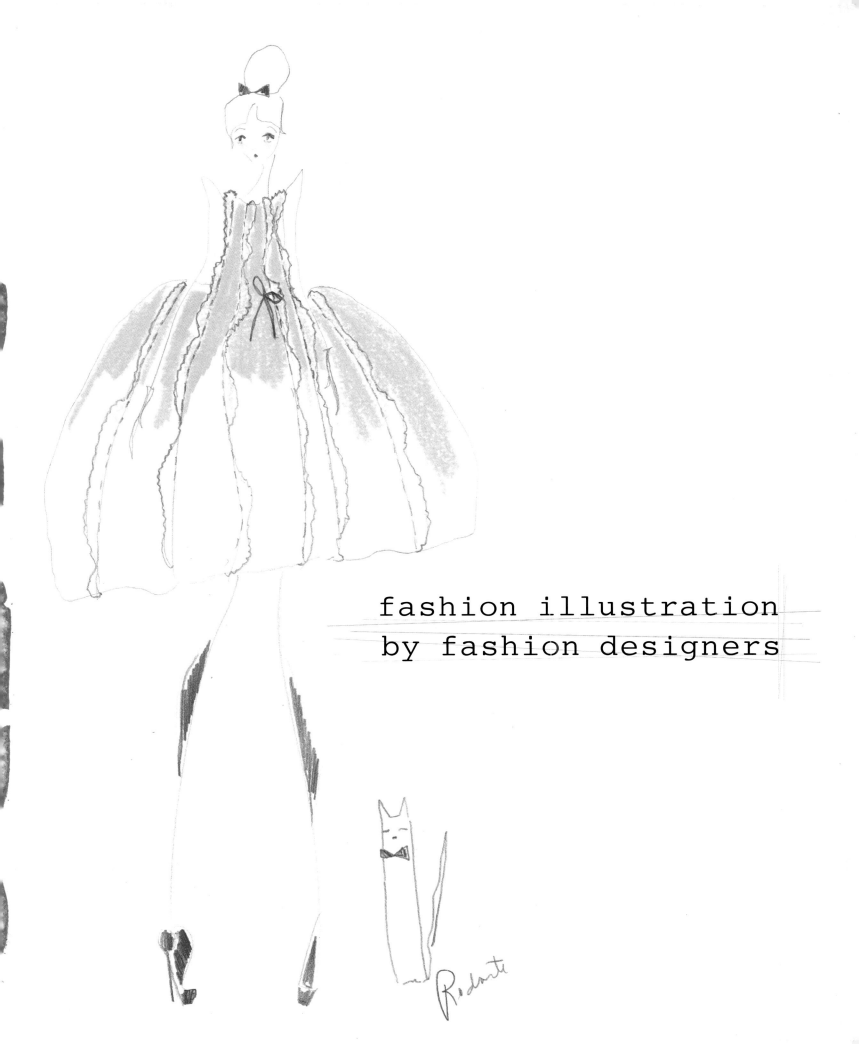

fashion illustration
by fashion designers

laird borrelli

fashion illustration
by fashion designers

with 280 illustrations, 200 in colour

Thames & Hudson

p. 1 Rodarte, colour pencil and ink on paper, 2007
p. 2 Molly Grad, watercolours, ink and pencil on
paper, 2005
Right: Gary Graham, gouache, pen and ink on paper,
Fall 2007

First published in the United Kingdom in 2008 by
Thames & Hudson Ltd, 181A High Holborn,
London WC1V 7QX

www.thamesandhudson.com

Fashion Illustration by Fashion Designers
© 2008 Thames & Hudson Ltd, London

All illustrations in this book are © the individual
fashion designer or fashion house

Reprinted 2009

British Library Cataloguing-in-Publication Data
A catalogue record for this book is available from
the British Library
ISBN 978-0-500-51397-2

Printed and bound in China by
C&C Offset Printing Co., Ltd.

contents

introduction

Christian Lacroix
Ink and watercolour on paper,
Haute couture Spring/Summer 2003

Ask a fashion designer to talk about fashion illustration, and you won't find them at a loss for words. Some will speak about the subject in almost mystical terms, while others rue the decline of the art (this book is – fortunately – vivid proof of the contrary).

Designers who draw tend to be fans of others who do too. Bruno Frisoni and Michael Vollbracht admit to admiring the nimble sketches of Yves Saint Laurent, while Igor Chapurin calls the dramatic work of the late Gianfranco Ferré out for praise. Egon Schiele and Antonio Lopez are perhaps the most popular icons among designers, though Christopher Kane adores the freedom of children's scribblings and Tsumori Chisato looks up to the mother of all Moomin trolls, Tove Jansson.

Drawing is not a requisite of the design process, of course. 'Fabric always comes first in design; drawing second. Remember Chanel never sketched,' Vollbracht reminds us. (Interestingly John Colapinto, in his 2007 *New Yorker* profile of Karl Lagerfeld, noted that the designer 'conceives his collections at a kind of platonic remove, in multicoloured drawings on paper, and only rarely touches fabric'.) One designer I asked to contribute to this book declined, exclaiming: 'I sketch, but so bad I almost don't dare to show to my assistants!'

A large part of the joy in making *Fashion Illustration by Fashion Designers* was the opportunity to interact with so many people I admire – and to be able to share with you their thoughts on my favourite subject.

This book is the third in my series on contemporary illustration, but it differs greatly from its siblings, as the contributors are working fashion designers rather than commercial illustrators. As such, the work that is presented here exists in an entirely different context to that which appeared in *Fashion Illustration Now* and *Fashion Illustration Next*.

Most of the work catalogued in those books was commissioned and intended for print in mainstream or corporate publications, or in advertising. And although many of those illustrators studied fashion, few actually practised it. The artists whose work appears in this publication, on the other hand, are an international cadre of fashion designers.

In order to contribute to this book, some designers untacked their artwork from inspiration boards; others ferreted their favourite sketches from messy piles in the corners of sunny ateliers bright with fabric and trimmings. Some drawings came with fabric samples stapled to them; others were scans pulled off a computer or retrieved from an organized filing system.

In some cases, designers – like New York creative Susan Cianciolo and Antwerp-based Christian Wijnants – sent us their priceless private sketchbooks. A number of artworks were also made expressly and generously for this book, and have never been seen before.

Whatever the living arrangements of a sketch before checking in for a stay *chez* the publisher, most were not intended for publication, but were working documents and highly personal – even intimate – forms of expression. Commercial illustrator-turned-designer Lovisa Burfitt is not alone in calling her drawings her 'babies'.

There is certainly an aspect of peepshow-like titillation to *Fashion Illustration by Fashion Designers* (though it is strictly PG) because these sketches were not intended for public viewing. 'Drawing,' explains Molly Grad, a Central Saint Martins graduate, 'is a direct handwriting; a way of seeing into a designer's thought processes.' The audience was originally either the designer him- or herself, or a design team, and the sketches were to be regarded as working documents to inspire and instruct design – not to be confused with their cousins, technical drawings (also known as croquis), which provide the exact information needed physically to make a collection.

Almost the only place the type of fashion drawing presented here is normally seen is in magazines, or inspiration stories in the fashion industry's daily newspaper *Women's Wear Daily* (*WWD*), or on websites such as Style.com. Part of the impetus behind this book has been to uncover and share the unsung and unseen art of illustration by fashion designers and to examine their personal design processes.

Much, though not all, of the work in this book has been done by hand. 'Drawing,' says London-based Antonio Ciutto, 'is the start of the physical process of realization.' This concentration on hand work stands in contrast to much of the work in my

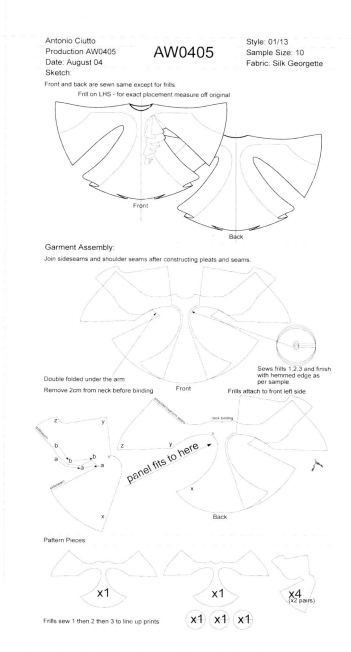

previous books, which – in keeping with the oldest tradition of fashion communications, mechanically produced plates, which date to the 1600s – is entirely conceived, or at least finished, on a machine, the final product then being delivered to the client as a digital file. (This production method, incidentally, throws the whole concept of what constitutes an original artwork into flux, especially as the end purpose of commercial fashion illustration is usually reproduction, but that is a discussion for another time.)

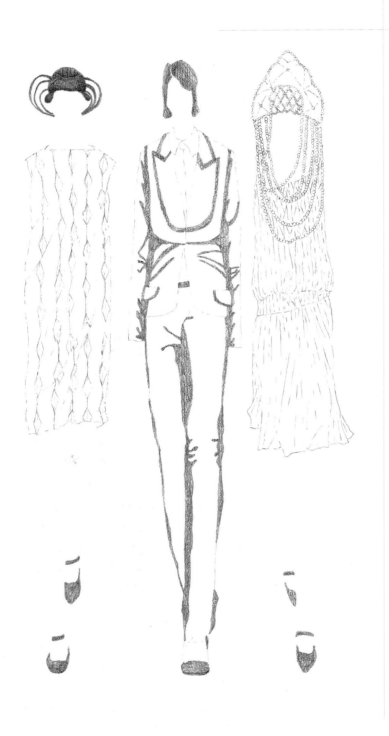

Alena Akhmadullina
Pencil on paper, Spring 2006

'I don't know what a computer is,' said one of the participants in this book – and she wasn't the only one. Fashion folk, generally speaking, have not been early adaptors in new technologies. But, for some, lo-fi is an active choice. 'I like being old-fashioned about drawings,' says Grad, whose preferred media are pencil and ink.

Frenchman Gilles Rosier, however, is open to new possibilities. 'I draw by hand ... for the moment!' he says. Bruno Basso and Christopher Brooke describe their work as 'a hybrid of traditional techniques and high technology'. Sonia Rykiel, the flame-haired Parisian knitwear designer, uses the computer for colouring, while Roksanda Ilincic, the Serbian-born and -trained designer, likes to combine digital work with hand-craft. Collage is a popular technique as well. 'The hand,' Ciutto concludes, is 'faster to get things out', but 'the computer helps in the seduction process'.

Since fashion photography marginalized the role of illustration in the late 1920s, the topic of man versus machine cannot be avoided. So I asked the contributors to this book what they thought a drawing could express that a photograph cannot. Outré Dutchman Bas Kosters replied, 'A drawing can create an intimate atmosphere with a tactile experience.' Antonio Berardi noted that 'a drawing is more pure and direct. It does not rely on tricks or technology and is perhaps the most sincere way of putting across an emotion.'

What do designers love about the art of drawing? Some value the ease and speed by which they are able to express their ideas. After all, sketches are a sort of manual download of brain to paper. 'It's easier to modify reality with a drawing,' says shoe wizard Bruno Frisoni. 'You can translate immediately what's in your head. It's sensual.'

Designers differ, however, in their perception of the relationship between the drawing and the final garment. For some a sketch is simply a starting point. 'The sketch is an idea, and intent,' states Christian Lacroix. 'A lot of them are like notes, or reminders, or like a gymnastic of the hand and spirit.' Moscow-based Denis Simachëv notes, 'Of course there is a relation between the drawing and the final garment, but the difference is extremely big. The drawing passes many levels

Bruno Frisoni for Roger Vivier
'London event'
Marker pen and coloured pencil
on paper, April 2006

Sonia Rykiel
Image created specially for
this publication
Ink on paper, 2007

of deformation. Life itself dictates which details should be changed.' 'For me,' states Hervé L. Leroux, 'a drawing represents only 10% of the final process. A good sketch does not always make a good dress. As far as I am concerned, the sketch is only a starter. The real life of a dress begins when you work with the fabric and volume in three dimensions.'

Ilincic, for one, is of another mind. 'The final garment is a three-dimensional drawing,' she says. 'I love observing this process – following the mood of the drawing being re-shaped into a real garment, becoming alive and starting a different life.' Zang Toi, a New Yorker by way of Malaysia, agrees: 'Almost all of the garments shown on my runway are almost 100% the way they appear in my sketches.' For Chapurin, the drawing and the garment 'are, as a rule, like twins'. And New Yorker Gary Graham chimes in, stating that in comparison to designing, 'the drawing process is often more interesting. The final garment is only one physical outcome of [the former].'

Is the pen mightier than the scissors? Many designers who draw seem to find some magic in the art in which the pen (or pencil, or mouse) assumes the role of medium through which intangible thoughts and emotions are translated into something articulate – and physical.

'I draw like I speak ... naturally,' Rykiel avers, but many designers will do hundreds of sketches before choosing one to pass on to the work-room. Howard Tangye, an artist and the head of womenswear design and drawing at his alma mater Central Saint Martins, even compares the practice of drawing to piano practice.

An important difference is that there are no notes to follow, no hips jutting in the wrong direction, no pesky gravity or hungry models to contend with: the only limits are the imagination and the paper's edge (though Rossella Tarabini admits to drawing on walls and tables and other strange places!). 'In my mind,' says Tangye, 'drawing is one of the designer's greatest tools. To be an excellent illustrator is quite something.'

Laird Borrelli, New York City

Fall 2007

Spring 2007

3.1 phillip lim

Looking back, Phillip Lim remembers drawing in kindergarten (his favourite subject then wasn't haute couture, but horses). These days Lim – who was born and trained in California and relocated to New York in 2004 to launch his own line – rapidly fills blank pages with simple linear images of dresses and coats and jackets, all drawn with his trusty, fine point, black ink Sharpie. Lim's first serious foray into the field of fashion drawing was as an assistant designer. 'I had to sketch to keep my job,' he explains. Now, with his star on the rise, his drawings play the role of 'road map to the final garment'. 'They're a sort of compass for the journey, if you will.'

Ink on paper, Spring 2007

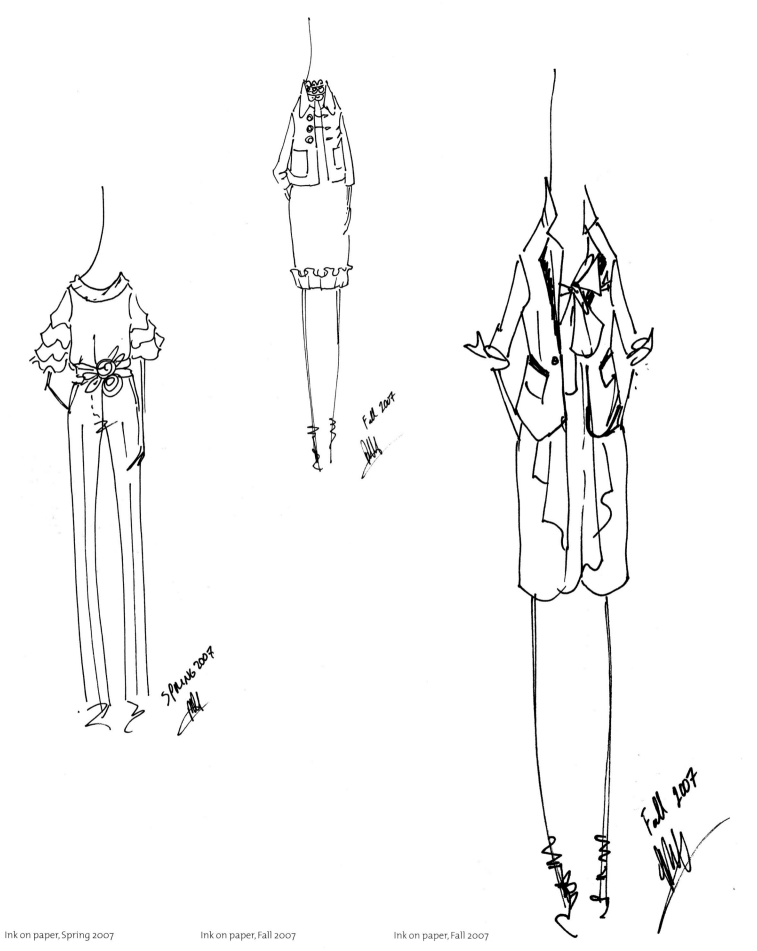

Ink on paper, Spring 2007   Ink on paper, Fall 2007   Ink on paper, Fall 2007

Ink on paper, Summer 2007

Ink on paper, Holiday 2006

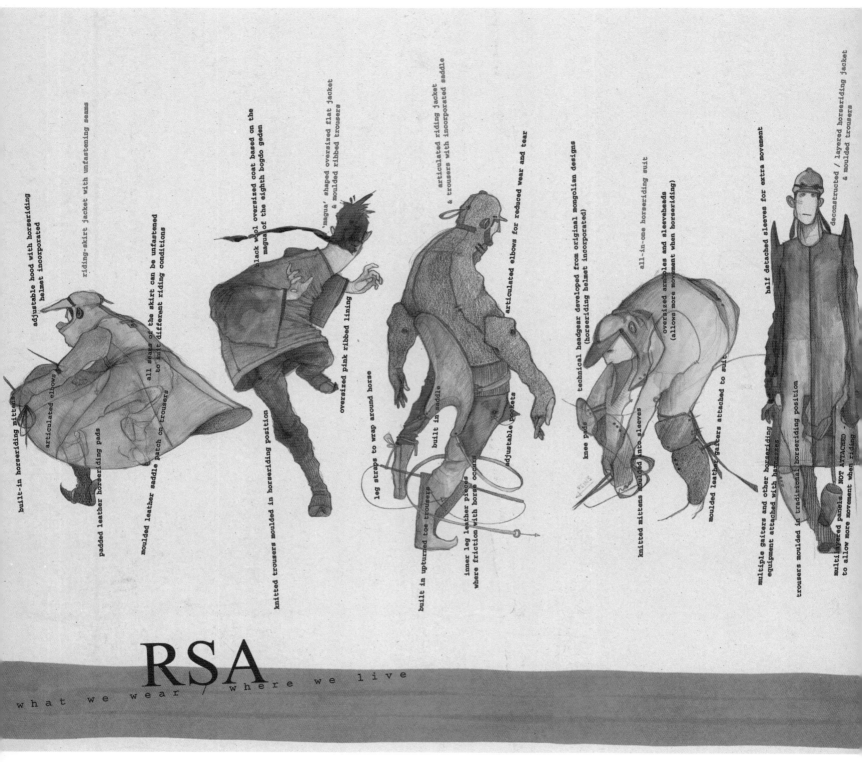

aitor throup

'As a child,' says Aitor Throup, 'I was constantly drawing the body in motion.' He still is. Raised in Argentina, Spain and England, the award-winning Royal College of Art graduate has a unique method of design that starts with the creation of a character. He makes a miniature sculpture of it, which he covers in fabric. 'I allow the darts and seams to be dictated by the structure itself,' he explains, 'so all my shirts, jackets, etc. look like generic garments at first, but on closer inspection, their construction lines are all equally distorted and seemingly misplaced.' Throup's goal in fashion design? 'To create three-dimensional, physical, wearable versions of my drawings/characters.'

'RSA DESIGN DIRECTIONS
What We Wear / Where We Live'
Pencils, watercolour, Magic Marker
(overlaid with computer typing), 2003

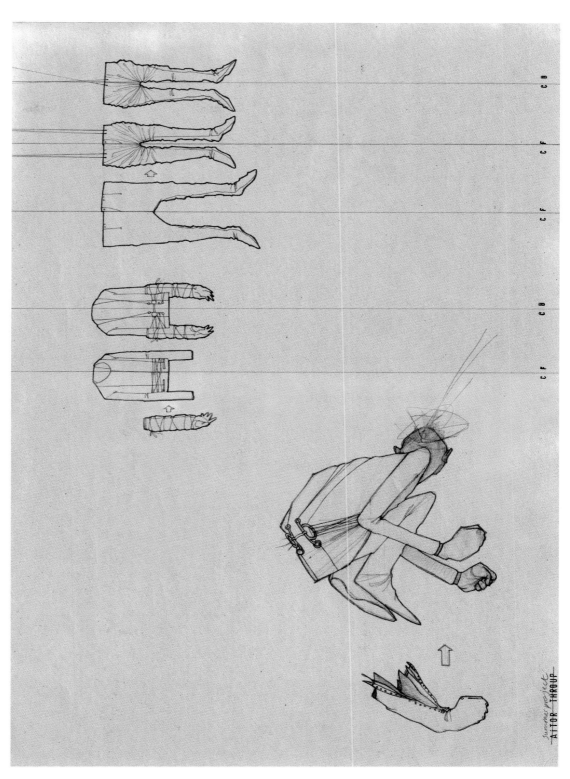

'Still Life #3'
Pencils, watercolour, stamps on
recycled paper, 2004

'Manchester 2'
Collage of pencil, watercolour, ink, fabric,
stamps and tape on various bits of paper
taped together, 2004

Above right and opposite
'Narasimha' drawings, from 'When
Football Hooligans Become Hindu Gods'
Pencil and watercolour on paper, 2006

Top
'Still Life # 16'
Pencils, watercolour, stamps on
recycled paper, 2004

Above
'Still Life # 8'
Pencils, watercolour, stamps on
recycled paper, 2004

alena akhmadullina

Alena Akhmadullina's first professional fashion drawings might have been made as a student at St Petersburg State University of Technology and Design, but long before that the designer was drawing princesses and their *toilettes*. 'It seems to me that the first act of creation in my childhood was ... a drawing,' she says. Akhmadullina has been presenting ready-to-wear collections since 2001, and in that time the role of drawings in her work has changed: over time they have become more like the looks that roll down her runway. 'Drawing is always a search,' she avers, 'an interweaving of reality and images that you have devised; it is the best fixation of an idea.'

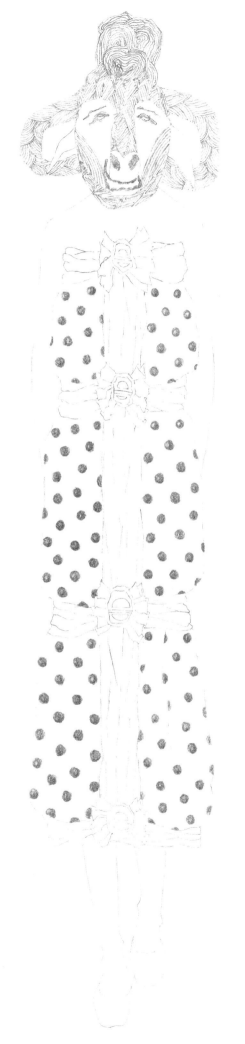

All images
Pencil on paper, Spring 2006

ANNA MOLINARI

Image created specially for this publication
Mixed media collage, Spring 2007

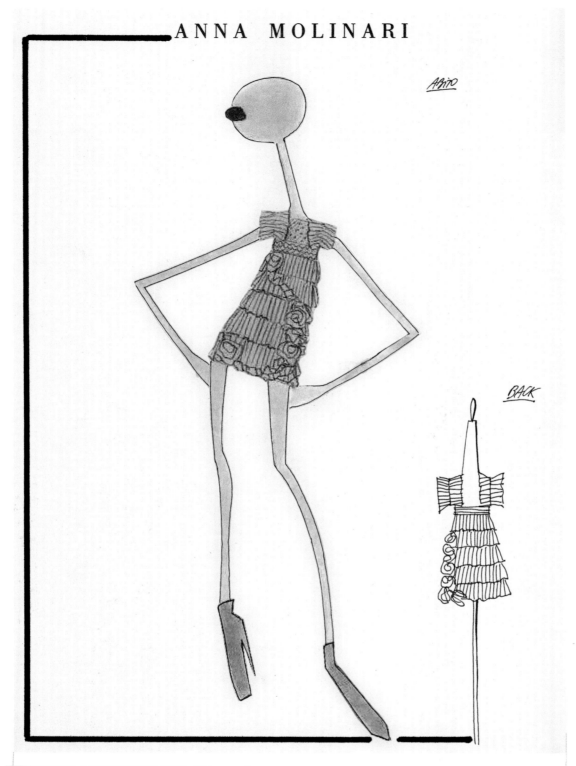

ABITO

BACK

anna molinari by rossella tarabini

Rossella Tarabini, who was born in Capri and trained as a fine artist in Italy and England, started designing
for Anna Molinari in 1995, after working for the family-owned Blumarine as art director. Drawing came
naturally to Tarabini, and on the job she still uses sketches to explain what she likes. She also acknowledges,
however, that the relationship between a drawing and a final garment can be a 'total dissociation'. 'Sometimes
from an amazing drawing what comes out is an unsatisfying dress,' she muses, 'while on other occasions
from unconvincing sketches you obtain nice and suitable garments.'

ANNA MOLINARI

PRIMAVERA ESTATE 2004

TACCO TRASPARENTE ???

Ink on paper, Spring 2004

'Portiere Dinotte'
Pencil, china ink, Pantone, pastel crayon,
tempera and watercolour on paper,
Fall/Winter 2004–2005

'Brancusi'
Pencil and Photoshop on paper,
Fall/Winter 2007–2008

antonio berardi

Prior to his apprenticeship with John Galliano, Antonio Berardi (a British designer with an Italian heritage, who graduated from London's Central Saint Martins) was learning about fashion from his older sister Piera. 'After seeing her illustrate, I would go off and try to emulate her work,' he says. 'Drawing is perhaps the most important aspect of my work. It is where I begin to define and fine-tune my ideas for the season, and creatively I find it to be meditative and stimulating at the same time.'

'Gypsy'
Pencil and Photoshop on paper,
Fall/Winter 2005–2006

'Religion'
Pencil, charcoal, tempera, pastel
crayon and china ink on paper,
Spring/Summer 2007

'Japan'
Pencil, charcoal, wax colours
and Photoshop on paper,
Spring/Summer 2007

'Bordello'
Adhesive colour paper and china ink
on paper, Spring/Summer 2003

'Les Incroyables'
Pencil and charcoal on paper,
Spring/Summer 2005

Sketchbook extract
Collage, pencil and watercolour,
Spring/Summer 2005

Sketchbook extract
Technical pen with black ink on tracing
paper, transferred to digital photograph,
2002, for Spring/Summer 2003

antonio ciutto

'I'm always drawing,' says Antonio Ciutto, the London-based South African who was designer-in-residence at the Victoria & Albert Museum in 2006. Ciutto, who trained as an architect before taking his Master's degree at Central Saint Martins, believes that a garment is but one 'physical outcome of the drawing process'. 'Drawing,' he says, 'is the start of the physical process of realization. It is for thinking and for technical resolution.'

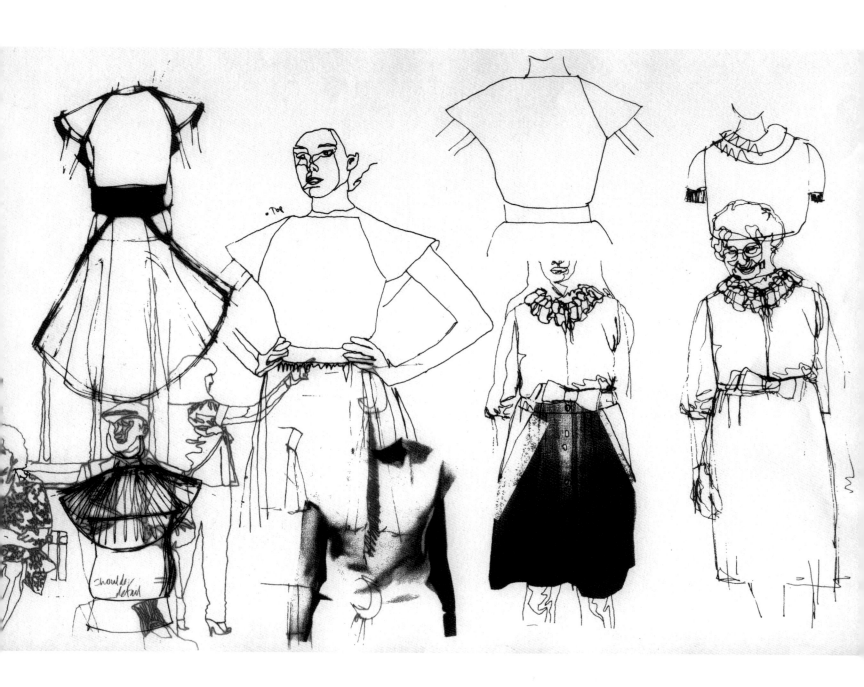

All images
Sketchbook sheets (from MA at
Central Saint Martins, London)
Technical pen with black ink on
tracing papers layered double and
photocopied, 2000

badgley mischka

'Other than searching for fabrics, sketching is always the first step in designing a new collection,' state Mark Badgley and James Mischka, who met as students at Parsons School of Design in New York, and joined forces in 1988. 'One zip and you're glamorous!' is how the duo like to describe their Old Hollywood-inspired work. It's not surprising, then, that Badgley's first memory of sketching fashion is 'watching TV and drawing Lucille Ball's dramatically shaped 1950s silhouettes'.

Ink on paper, Spring 2006   Ink on paper, Spring 2006

'US-Visit'
Coloured ink and pencil on paper,
September 2006

Untitled
Acrylic and coloured ink with collage
technique on paper, January 2006

bas kosters

Illustrator, (performance) artist, punk musician – Dutch designer Bas Kosters is an award-winning graduate of the Fashion Institute Arnhem, for whom drawing is an important, if not the first, step in the design process. Drawings, he believes, have the ability to 'create an intimate atmosphere with a tactile experience'. Not one for subtlety, Kosters, who aims to tell stories through his clothing, believes that 'a grand gesture makes your message all the clearer'. As he asserts, 'I like clear communication.'

'Sex, Crime and Suspense'
Pencil and ballpoint on paper,
Autumn 2003

basso & brooke

Bruno Basso, a Brazilian graphic designer, and Christopher Brooke, a graduate of Kingston University and Central Saint Martins, joined forces in 2003 and soon after won the 2004 Fashion Fringe prize with their audacious print-based collection. 'Drawing is the vehicle for the big picture,' says Brooke. 'It's the stage of the design process when you can express volume and silhouette without limitations. I always hope that the final garment encompasses the emotional feeling that the illustration holds.'

All images
'The Garden of Earthly Delights'
Ink on paper, digitally colourized,
Spring/Summer 2005

'The Garden of Earthly Delights'
Ink on paper, digitally colourized,
Spring/Summer 2005

'The Garden of Earthly Delights'
Pencil on paper, Spring/Summer 2005

'Vanity Affair'
Ink on paper, digitally colourized,
Spring/Summer 2006

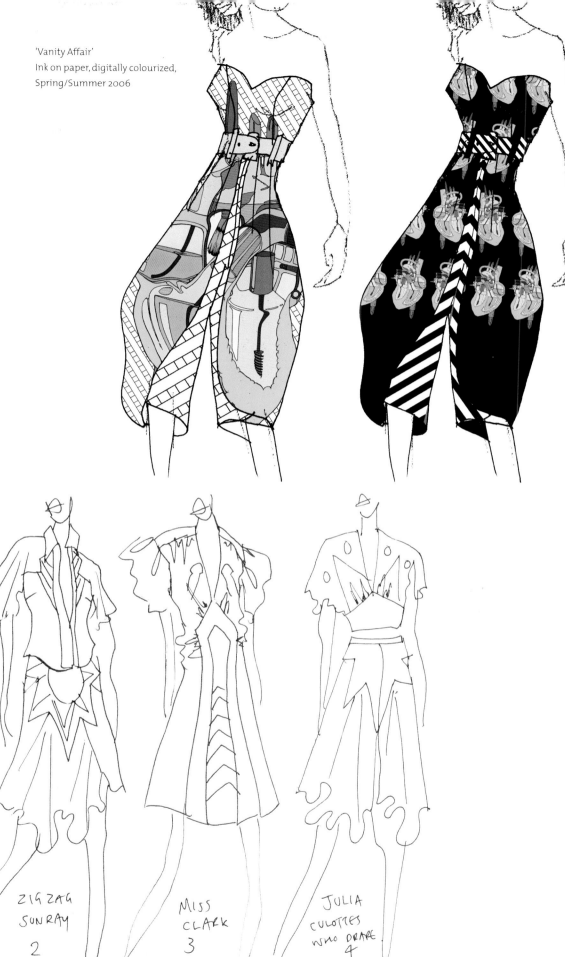

MADAME
PANEL
SKIRT
1

ZIG ZAG
SUNRAY
2

MISS
CLARK
3

JULIA
CULOTTES
WHO DRAPE
4

'I ♥ Roses'
Computer-enhanced
drawing, 2006

'Hey! Thights-Knee-Highs-
Stockings + Sock It To Me!'
Computer-enhanced
drawing, 2004

betsey johnson

'Drawing,' says the legendary Betsey Johnson (Edie Sedgwick was her house model in the 1960s), 'has always been a big part of my fashion design world. I do all the visuals for the company: I draw the designs, the ads, mailers, showroom art, and fashion drawings of each collection.' Born in Connecticut and educated at the Pratt Institute and Syracuse University, Johnson is the youngest designer ever to receive the Coty Award (1972), and in 1999 the Council of Fashion Designers of America created the Timeless Talent Award specifically for her. Drawing, she says, allows you to 'highlight important elements of design by exaggeration'.

'Peace On Your Earth'
Marker on paper, 1990s

Marker and crayon on paper,
1967

Opposite page
'Proust's Skirt – An Invisible City'
Collage, pencil, pen, ink, inkjet,
Letraset and Photoshop on
French accountancy paper,
Autumn/Winter February 2006

'Butterfly Bike City – A dream
sequence in order'
Collage, pencil, pen, ink, inkjet,
Letraset and Photoshop on paper,
Couture 01 January 2007

'Forever – A dream sequence
in order'
Collage, pencil, pen, ink, inkjet,
Letraset and Photoshop on paper,
Couture 01 January 2007

how can we go where we once went?

boudicca

'There is no greater reward than seeing an actual rendering of an imagined idea,' state Brian Kirkby and Zowie
Broach, the esoteric husband-and-wife team behind the British label named after an ancient warrior queen.
Their collections – which grow from 'seed' drawings – are conceived of as 'stories, short scenes from films, that
at times are simple and reference the obvious, at others become complex and ill fitting'. Drawing, they say, is
'the purest form of communication'. 'It is our earliest form of language ... the major printer of the imagination.
We are both students of the language of imagination.'

For here the day unravels what the night has woven —PROUST

BOUDICCA

Bruno Frisoni collection
Marker pen and coloured pencil
on paper, Spring/Summer 2007

bruno frisoni

Born in Italy and raised in France, Bruno Frisoni worked at Christian Lacroix and Jean-Louis Scherrer prior to launching his own line in 1999. He was named creative director of Roger Vivier in 2002. Frisoni draws by hand – 'the right one!' His shoe collections begin with drawings of fashion silhouettes, for which he then imagines the appropriate accessories. 'Generally, I need the drawing to please me to be able to work,' Frisoni says. 'I consider my work done when the piece realized is almost like the drawing.'

Á las là
Jésuis à
l'aise —

Bruno Frisoni for Roger Vivier
Marker pen and coloured pencil
on paper, Spring/Summer 2004

Bruno Frisoni collection
Marker pen and coloured pencil on
paper, Autumn/Winter 2007–2008

Bruno Frisoni collection
Marker pen and coloured pencil on
paper, Autumn/Winter 2007–2008

Bruno Frisoni for Roger Vivier
Marker pen and coloured pencil
on paper, Spring/Summer 2006

Bruno Frisoni for Roger Vivier
Marker pen and coloured pencil
on paper, Spring/Summer 2004

Ink on paper,
Spring/Summer 2002

bruno pieters

With a drawing 'you can create something new that doesn't exist' says Bruno Pieters, a graduate of Antwerp's Royal Academy of Fine Arts. Pieters, who originally wanted to be a painter, debuted his eponymous ready-to-wear line in 2002. He was awarded the Stella Contemporary Fashion Award in 2006, and in 2007 won the ANDAM award and was appointed art director of Hugo for Hugo Boss. 'I never do technical drawings,' he says. 'I design the whole look how it should be.'

Ink on paper,
Spring/Summer 2004

S/S 2004

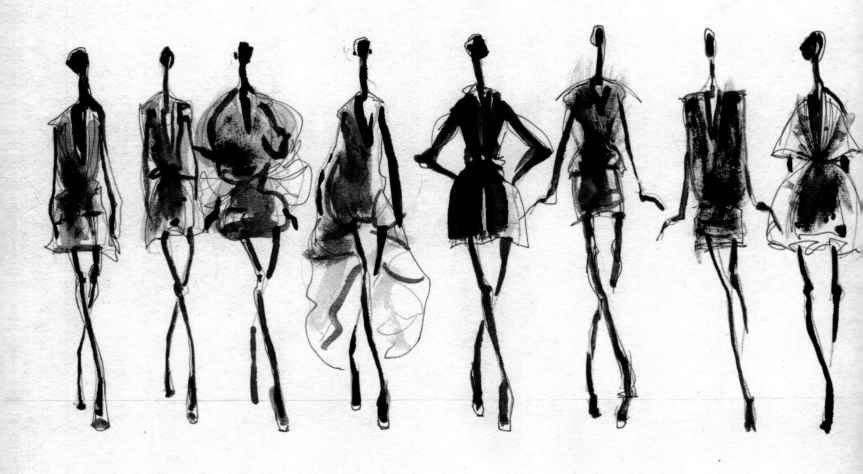

Ink on paper, 2001

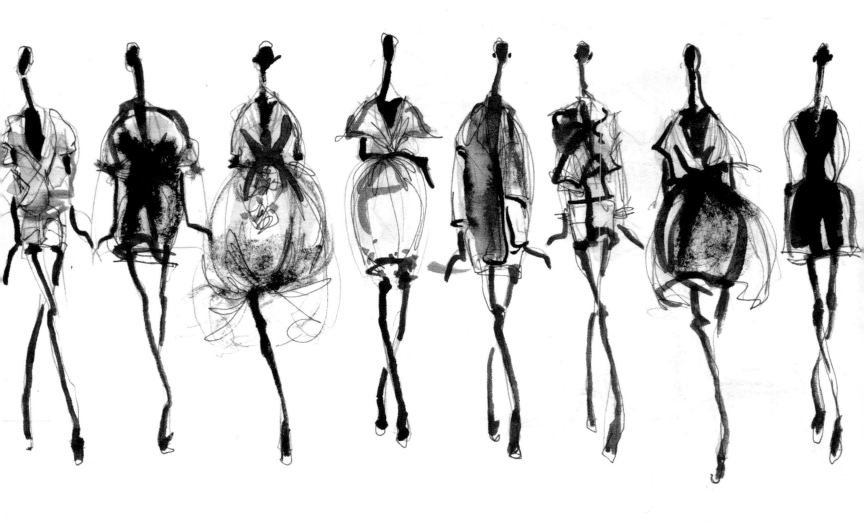

All images
'People Have The Power'
Pencil, ink with brush, coloured pencil and
felt pen on paper, Spring/Summer 2007

burfitt

Lovisa Burfitt, who studied at Beckmans College of Fashion and the Royal College of Art in Stockholm, was an esteemed commercial illustrator prior to her career in fashion design, which officially began in Paris in 2003, when she teamed up with Kajsa Leanderson and launched Burfitt, a line of clothing featuring her artwork. Making comparisons with her fashion drawings, Burfitt describes the more free, note-like sketches she makes when starting to design a collection as 'quite horrible' (we beg to differ). Be it a considered work or a scribble, 'for me,' Burfitt exclaims, '[drawing] is really an adrenalin shot!'

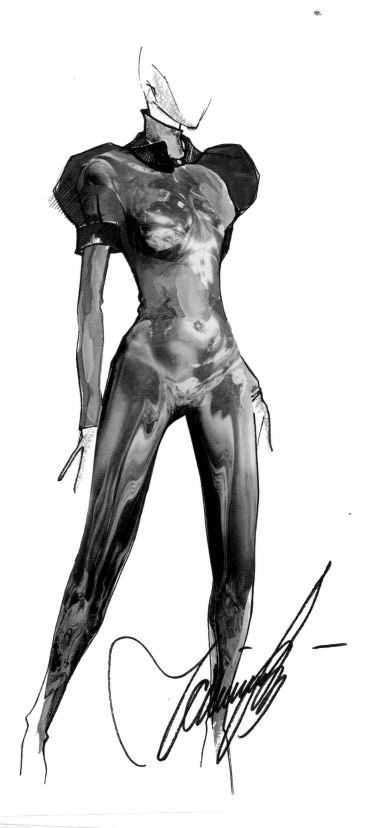

chapurin

Although Igor Chapurin grew up in an artistic household in Belarus, he didn't start sketching fashion until he was in the army. 'I think it is due to my being completely stripped of any visual beauty ... [that] a strong desire to bring it about with my own means was born in my inner self,' he explains. After winning a Nina Ricci competition in Paris in 1992, Chapurin's business developed from couture into readywear, accessories, home, ski and children's wear. Though he has many sketches to make, while he is drawing, Chapurin says, 'I am both accurate and relaxed at the same time – accurate conceptually, relaxed in my creativity.'

Ink on paper, Winter 2007   Ink on paper, Spring 2007

Ink on paper, Prêt-à-porter
Spring/Summer 1989

Opposite
Ink on paper, Prêt-à-porter
Fall/Winter 1999–2000

christian lacroix

'I never learned to draw,' Christian Lacroix says, 'but as far as I remember, I always had a pad and a pencil. Drawing is such a habit, a need, a reflex, that even without any paper or pen I can draw with my finger an invisible sketch in the air, or with a piece of wood, a straw or a stone on sand or mud....' Born in Arles, Lacroix moved to Paris with the intention of becoming a museum curator, but fate intervened and he ended up designing clothes for the house of Jean Patou before starting his own label in 1987. He says that he sketches all the time. 'This is my way of taking notes, imagining my ideal of a world, [and] trying on different moods before illustrating for real.'

Christian Lacroix Paris Att. 205/2000 [signature]

Ink and watercolour on paper,
Haute couture Spring/Summer 2003

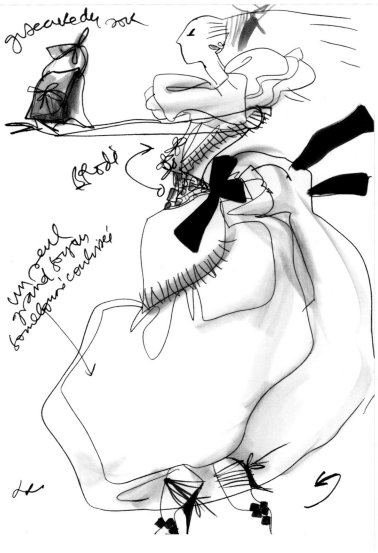

Ink and watercolour on paper,
Haute couture Spring/Summer 2007

Ink and watercolour on paper,
Haute couture Spring/Summer 2003

Ink and watercolour on paper,
Haute couture Spring/Summer 2003

Images created specially for this publication
Pencil on paper, 2007

christian wijnants

Growing up in Brussels with an art-teacher grandmother, Christian Wijnants was interested in art long before
he enrolled at the Royal Academy of Fine Arts in Antwerp and started winning awards for his designs. Wijnants
builds his collections slowly, explaining that he needs 'first to create an atmosphere, to define a universe, with mood-
boards and cuttings'. The drawings – by hand – follow. 'Your hand senses emotions, doubts, irregularities on paper.
I love that direct contact from the body to the paper. It can have something very sensual or very raw. Depending on
your mood, your breath, the touch of the pencil will be different and will influence the drawing.'

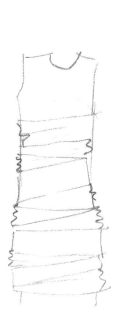

'(Multicolour) knitwear study'
Coloured pencil on paper, Spring 2005

Pen and pencil on paper, June 2006

Pen and pencil on paper, 2004

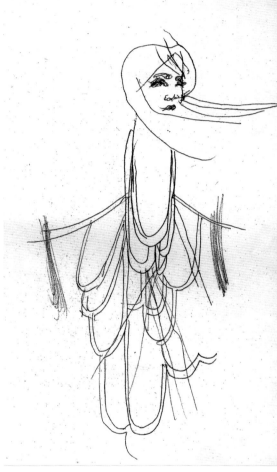

christopher kane

'I recall doodling and sketching women with and without clothes at around four or five years old. I used to fantasize about ballgowns with bows and long-haired girls.' A Scotsman whose MA collection at Central Saint Martins was sponsored by Donatella Versace, Christopher Kane won the Harrods Design Award in 2006 and was named Scottish Designer of the Year. What's the role of sketching in his work? 'The initial drawings get me excited and ready to start creating clothes.'

Pen and pencil on paper, 2004

Pen and pencil on paper, 2005

costello tagliapietra

'It's really important for us to think the garment out on paper,' explain Jeffrey Costello and Robert Tagliapietra, the Brooklyn-based design duo. The two learned to sew from their respective grandmothers (both of whom had worked for Norman Norell). Tagliapietra, who trained as a painter, only began to sketch fashion after beginning to collaborate with Costello, who had been designing for musicians and actors. 'The funny thing is,' they say, 'that all of our illustrations are in black and white, never colour. This may be because colour is really important to us, and we work best later in the toile stage draping the colours rather than trying to paint them....'

Pencil on paper, Spring 2007

denis simachëv

The first step Russian designer Denis Simachëv takes when designing clothes is to make a drawing. But that drawing, in the course of being made three-dimensional, 'passes many levels of deformation'. 'Life itself,' he says, 'dictates which details should be changed.' A well-rounded talent who studied art, graphics and décor before graduating from the Textile Academy in Moscow, Simachëv then took courses in Spain, which were followed by advertising and directing classes at the Russian Institute of Cinema. As he says, 'Drawing gives an opportunity to embody exactly an idea from your mind at the moment that it happens.'

All images
'Chukotka'
Pencil on paper, Fall/Winter 2006–2007

All images
'Chukotka'
Pencil on paper, Fall/Winter 2006–2007

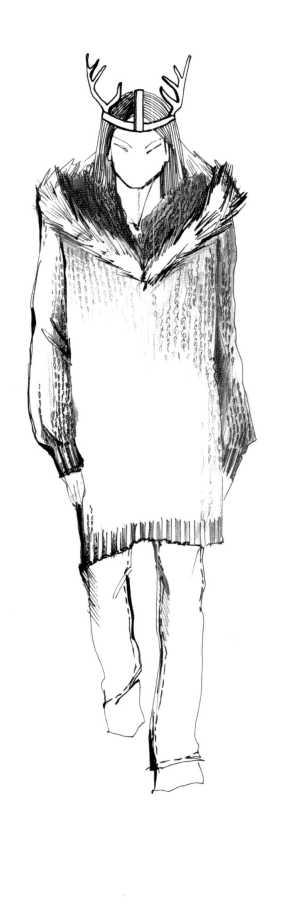

doo.ri

'Sew, schlep and sketch' is how Doo-Ri Chung has jokingly described her daily routine. A Parsons grad, she worked as head designer at Geoffrey Beene before going solo in 2001, working from the basement of her parents' dry-cleaning business. Five years later she won the 2006 Vogue/CFDA Fashion Fund Award. 'There is immense freedom with drawing,' Chung notes. 'There are no boundaries and the only limitation exists within one's own imagination.'

Ink and coloured pencil on paper,
Spring 2007

Mixed media collage, Fall 2006

Ink and coloured pencil on paper,
Spring 2006

Ink on paper, Fall 2006

Ink and coloured pencil on paper,
Fall 2007

Mixed media on paper, Spring 2007

Ink and coloured pencil on paper,
Spring 2007

elise øverland

As a child, the Norwegian-born Elise Øverland used to lie under her bed with a flashlight and draw on the bed-boards. 'It was secret,' she says. Her talent is very visible these days among the fashion cognoscenti and the rock crowd, whom she outfits for tours. Øverland studied business at the University of San Francisco Academy of Art College and design at New York's Parsons School of Design. 'Drawing is my inner landscape turned out in the pencil,' she explains. 'In a drawing you can see the line quality as a fine woven proof or reflection of your soul's state of mind: bold, thick lines of anger, or weak, neurotic lines that a photo can't reproduce.'

'Norwicket'
Pencil on paper, 2004

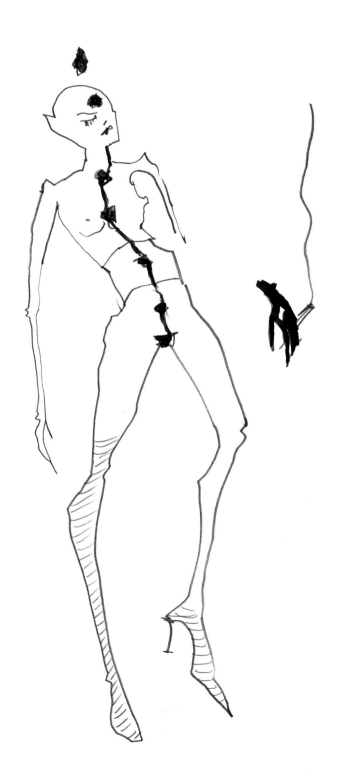

WHAT I WANT TO WEAR FOR MY PRESENTATION

Untitled
Pencil and watercolour, 2006

'What I Want to Wear For My Presentation'
Pencil on paper, 2007

'Darwin print dress'
Collage, gouache, pen and ink
on paper, Fall 2007

'Rope jacket'
Gouache, pen and ink on paper,
Fall 2007

'Wool jacket, skirt and slip'
Gouache, pen and ink on paper,
Fall 2004

gary graham

Gary Graham, who grew up in Delaware, says, 'I would draw Vargas girls' legs when I was little, and thought
if I could draw them perfectly then I would know how to draw.' He went on to study at the Art Institute of
Chicago, and established his line in 1999. As his business grows, Graham finds himself sketching more. 'In the
beginning I would do all of the draping by myself, so I wouldn't draw much,' he explains. 'There is so much
design that happens when working on the dress form that most of my initial sketches have nothing to do with
the final design ... but this process is changing and I am starting to work more ideas out two-dimensionally.'

generra by pina ferlisi

Growing up in Canada, Pina Ferlisi 'became fascinated with how expressive a drawing could be, and how I could change the mood of my character with the stroke of a pencil'. Since then this graduate of Ontario's Sheridan College has changed more than moods: she helped launch the Marc by Marc Jacobs label, and headed the design team at The Gap, before becoming the creative director of Generra in 2006. When sketching, Ferlisi first draws by hand and then uses the computer for enhancement. 'I usually have a certain girl in mind for a season,' she says. 'My sketches become the vehicle for my muse.'

All images
Mixed media on paper,
Spring/Summer 2007

Pencil and ink on paper,
Spring 2007

Pencil and ink on paper,
Fall 2007

giambattista valli

Born in Rome, Giambattista Valli lives and works in Paris, where he has been designing his own line since 2005. Valli studied fashion at the European Design Institute in Rome and illustration at Central Saint Martins in London, before gaining experience at Roberto Capucci, Fendi, Krizia and Emanuel Ungaro. Valli is fascinated by women – 'the way they walk, their attitudes, their silhouettes'. His ideal woman? 'An eclectic one.'

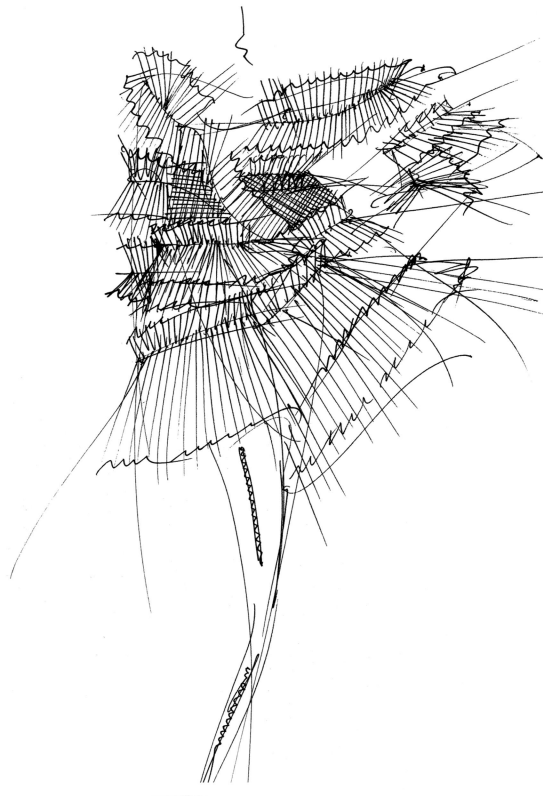

gianfranco ferré

'I could never envision an immobile dress hanging on a hanger,' the leonine Italian designer Gianfranco Ferré once admitted. 'A silhouette captured in its essential points – the shoulders, the waist and the legs that extend down the sheet of the paper – is composed of but a few strokes of the pencil, but it is already a human figure.' Before he moved to Paris to work for himself and, for a time, Christian Dior, Ferré trained as an architect at the Polytechnic in Milan, where he honed his sketching skills. 'Drawing,' he said, before his untimely death in 2007, 'is a timeless love that I have stayed true to for almost forty years.'

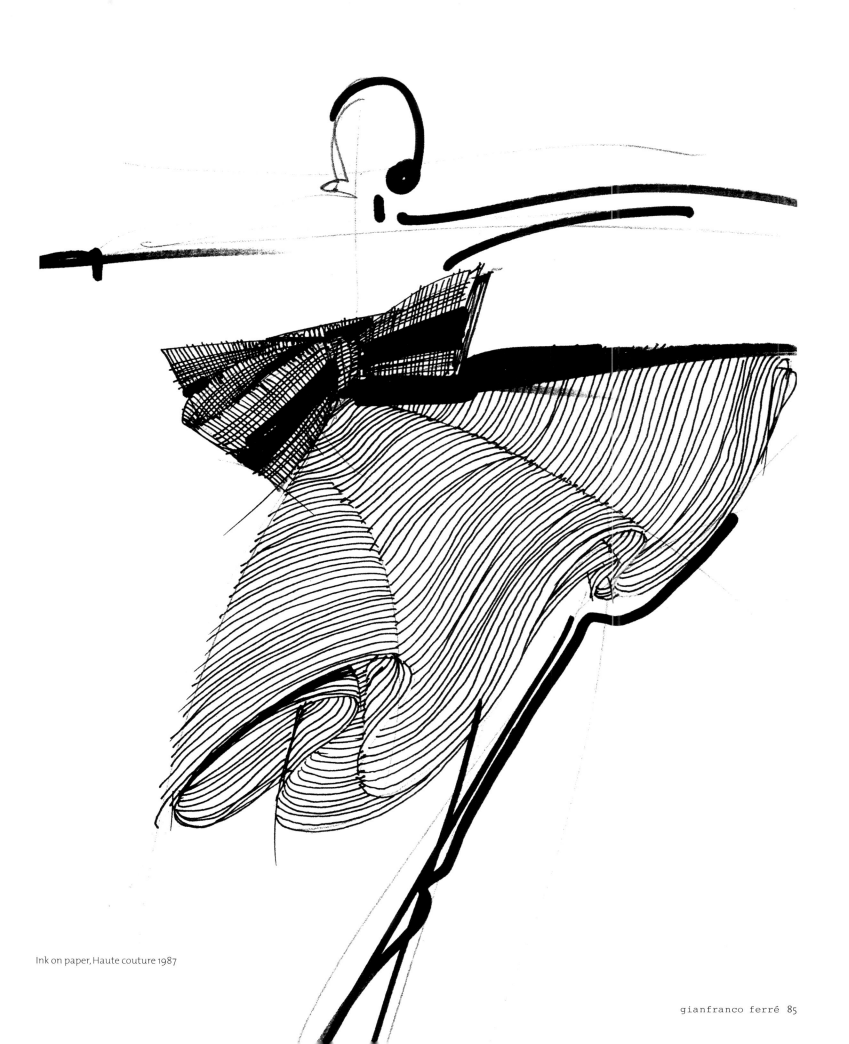

Ink on paper, Haute couture 1987

Ink on paper, Fall 1989

Ink on paper, Spring 2002

GIANFRANCO
FERRE

GIANFRANCO
FERRE

Ink on paper, Spring 1997   Ink on paper, Spring 2002

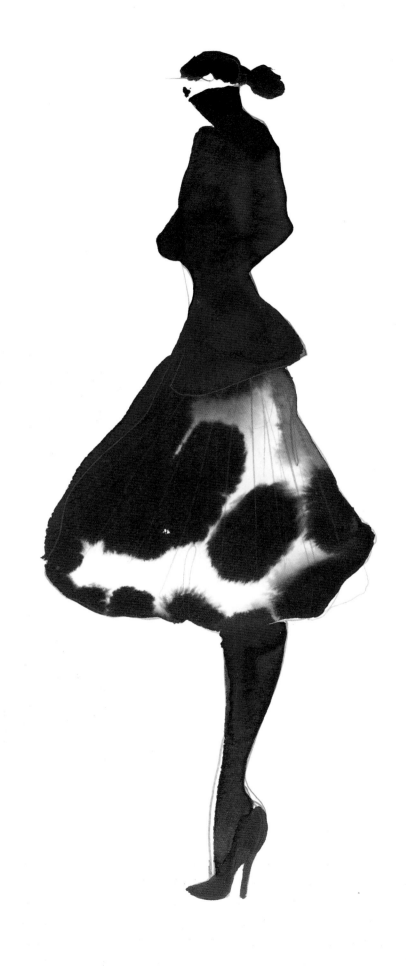

Opposite page
'Kid A'
Watercolour ink on paper, 2006

'Kid B'
Watercolour ink on paper, 2006

'Kid C'
Watercolour ink on paper, 2006

giles

'Drawing functions in my life in many ways,' says Central Saint Martins graduate Giles Deacon. 'It's a form of relaxation and a route for escape. I try to draw for at least half an hour every day.' Deacon, who went solo in 2005 – and was named creative director of Daks a year later – gathered work experience at Jean-Charles de Castelbajac and Bottega Veneta, among other places. 'The beauty I find with drawing,' he says, 'is it places you in a time where you don't have to think, "Oh, I've got to design now", but you can start doing some drawings and then after twenty minutes of getting lost in that world it can start turning into something that you've never even imagined.'

Tank top
with A Stripes

Beige
Safari
Jacket with
belt crisscrossing
at the back

Black ivoryVichy
Jacket with
spikes and
OBI-tie at the
back

Tea note Silk
Skirt with
Black Elastic band

high waisted slim
pants

Tribe Collection

Spring/Summer
04
Shirts & Collars
in Motion

'Tribe'
Pencils, pen and ink on paper,
Spring/Summer 2007

'Shirts and Collars in Motion'
Pencils, pen and ink on paper,
Spring/Summer 2004

'Controversy'
Pencils, pen and ink on paper,
Spring/Summer 2006

gilles rosier

'I think that one of the reasons I do my job is because I love to draw,' admits Gilles Rosier, the Parisian designer
who worked with Guy Paulin, Christian Dior and Kenzo, among others, before going out on his own in 2004.
'I consider that the garment must be as good-looking as the drawing – or even better,' he says. 'Because my
fashion is about attitude and movement, I sketch in the garment a certain gesture that I try to build and make
as close as possible to my original drawings.'

'Stabat Anima'
Pencils, pen and ink on paper,
Winter 2006

'Tribe'
Pencils, pen and ink on paper,
Spring/Summer 2007

'Tribe'
Pencils, pen and ink on paper,
Spring/Summer 2007

'Kiss of the Dragonfly'
Pencils, pen and ink on paper,
Spring/Summer 2005

'Shirts and Collars in Motion'
Pencils, pen and ink on paper,
Spring/Summer 2004

givenchy by riccardo tisci

'I am very romantic and sometimes very dark,' says Riccardo Tisci, who has designed for the house of Givenchy since 2005. Born in Lombardy, Tisci is the lastborn of nine children – and the only boy. He graduated from Central Saint Martins in London, and then worked in Germany for Puma, and in Italy for Coccapani, Ruffo Research and his own line before taking the job in Paris. 'People call me a Gothic designer,' he told *The New York Times*'s Cathy Horyn. 'I don't think I am....' But he has to admit: 'I like black, I like white. I never like what's in the middle.'

'Sirena'
Pencil and ink on paper,
'La Sirène' collection,
Haute couture Spring 2007

'Johas'
Pencil and ink on paper,
Prêt-à-porter Fall 2007

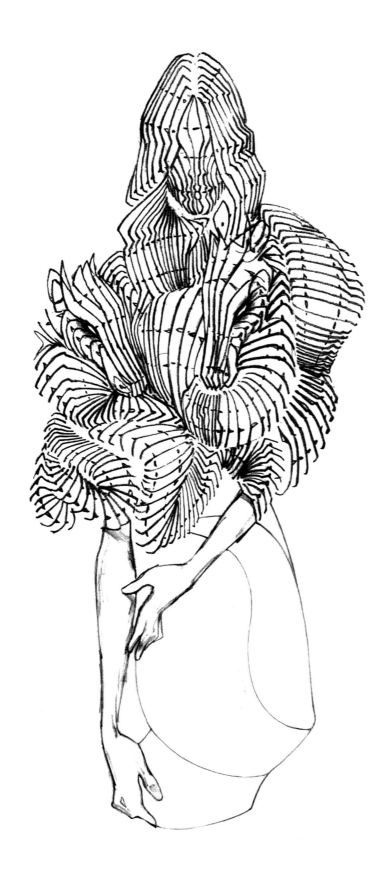

Pencil on paper,
'Mappemonde' collection,
Haute couture Fall 2006

gustavo arango

Gustavo Arango was born in Colombia and raised in Puerto Rico. Fashion brought him to New York, where he studied at the Fashion Institute of Technology, and then to Paris, where he worked as an assistant designer at Pierre Balmain. These days Arango designs his own line, working between San Juan and Manhattan. 'I need to be in a certain mood to draw,' he explains. 'I need to be motivated – inspired by something.'

All images created specially
for this publication
Pencil, markers and watercolour
on paper, March 2007

Both images created specially
for this publication
Pencil, markers and watercolour
on paper, March 2007

'The Exquisite Corpse'
Japanese calligraphy pen
and Photoshop on paper,
March 2007

hall ohara

Hall Ohara is the offspring of Central Saint Martins graduates Steven Hall, from England, and Yurika Ohara, from Japan. The two fell in love on the course and were married a year before starting their label in 2005. 'Drawing is something that has fascinated me since I can remember,' says Ohara, whose sketches are often incorporated as prints into Hall Ohara collections. All the work on these pages was made by her. 'Drawings can express focal points on an extreme level,' she says, 'and at the same time still provide individualistic expression.'

'Joy + Love = Perfect'
Japanese calligraphy pen, pastels,
crayons and oil colour pencils on
paper, May 2003

'Leaving Monochrome Behind'
Japanese calligraphy pen and
Photoshop on paper, October 2006

'Spur of the Moment'
Japanese calligraphy pen and
Photoshop on paper, March 2007

hanuk

Hanuk Kim, the Korean-born, New York-based designer, was educated at the Fashion Institute of Design and Merchandising, the Academy of Art College in San Francisco, and Parsons School of Design in New York and Paris. Kim worked with Patrick Robinson and Narciso Rodriguez before launching his own accessories in 2000 and womenswear in 2004. 'When I see details ... I draw them,' he says. 'I usually have a sketchbook with me all the time. Sometimes I like to rip a page out as a thank-you note, etc. It's like giving part of you away – in a good way.'

All images
Gouache, ink and pencil, Spring 1995

Both images
Pencil and ink on paper, Winter 2006

robe en Fente

hervé l. leroux

'I think I am a self-taught designer.... What I call the "monkey" way. It means learning from looking at other works,' says Hérve L. Leroux, *né* Léger, self-deprecatingly. Leroux, who worked with Tan Guidicelli and Karl Lagerfeld, went solo in 1985 and became known for his form-fitting 'bandage' dresses. He might do a thousand sketches for a collection of a hundred pieces, but, 'as far as I am concerned,' he says, 'the sketch is only a starter. The real life of a dress begins when you work with the fabric and the volume in three dimensions.'

Isaac Mizrahi for Target
'Striped cotton handknit sweater;
denim jeans'
Ink and coloured pencil on paper,
Fall 2003

Isaac Mizrahi for Target
'Pink canvas hunting jacket; black
cashmere crewneck; black corduroy
jeans; pointed sneakers'
Ink and coloured pencil on paper,
Fall 2003

S T R A P L E S S
C A S H M E R E
K I L T

LINDA
Fall 89

62

1982

'Strapless cashmere kilt gown'
Graphite, coloured pencil, watercolour
and swatches on paper, Fall 1989

'Double-breasted trench coats'
Graphite, coloured pencil and
watercolour on paper, 1982

Black Cashmere crewneck.

Pink Canvas Hunting Jacket (with quilted lining, corduroy collar, reinforced-stitched elbows.)

Cotton handknit sweater.

Black Corduroy Jeans.

Pointed sneakers

isaac mizrahi

'I make a wish when I sketch, and it comes out as a drawing,' says the Brooklyn-born designer Isaac Mizrahi, who studied acting at the High School of Performing Arts in New York before pursuing a degree in fashion from Parsons School of Design. Parallel to his own line, Mizrahi has been designing for the mass retailer Target since 2003. 'Some things I draw exactly,' he says. 'I know exactly what they'll look like in the end. Other things evolve from the drawing. I'm very old-fashioned in that way. Design happens in fittings as a response to the attitude of a sketch. And if sometimes the final garment does not look like the drawing, it always "feels" like the sketch.'

NACMI #46

74

Cordula

'Linen and ribbon "X" dress'
Ink, graphite and watercolour on
paper, Spring 1990

'Black-white stripe double-face satin
smock; black sheer opaque jumpsuit'
Ink, graphite, watercolour and
swatches on paper, Fall 1989

Images created specially
for this publication
Paper collage, 2007

james thomas

Born in Britain and trained at London's Royal College of Art, James Thomas now lives in the United States.
'I started to make fashion drawings five years after I learned to talk,' says the designer, a Calvin Klein alumnus.
Thomas makes speed sketches with thick nib markers or ink, but he also likes the paper-cut method. 'It's a
style of working in which accidents can happen. That's the important moment in the design process for me.'

Images created specially
for this publication
Paper collage, 2007

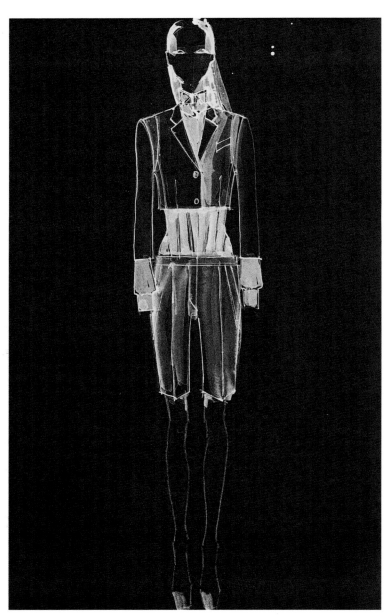 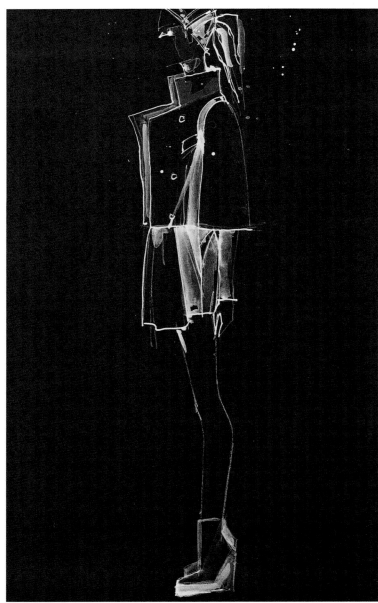

jens laugesen

Jens Laugesen was born in Denmark and now lives in London, where he designs his own line and teaches at Central Saint Martins – from whose Masters course he graduated with distinction in 2002. Prior to that, he received a design degree from the Chambre Syndicale de la Couture Parisienne and a Masters in Fashion Management from the Institut Français de la Mode. If a drawing is 'the aspiration, the dream, the starting point, the only way of explaining a vision', Laugesen asserts, 'the final garment is always better, simply because it is properly thought through – more realistic, and not an illustration of an idea.'

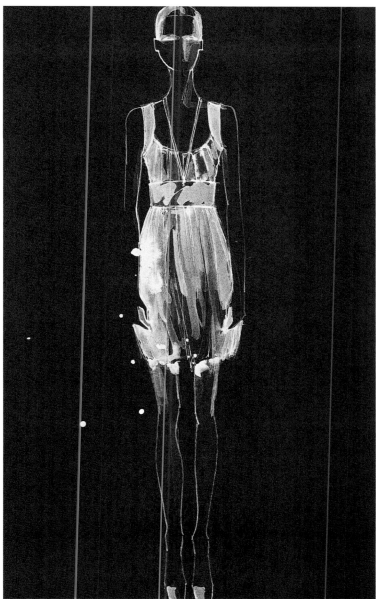

'Future Now 03/01'
Indian ink on paper, June 2006

'Future Now 03/02'
Indian ink on paper, June 2006

'Future Now 03/03'
Indian ink on paper, June 2006

'Future Now 03/04'
Indian ink on paper, June 2006

'Day skirtsuit from the centennial
anniversary of Georg Jensen'
Pencil, colour crayons, pastel
and Pantone marker on paper,
Spring/Summer 2003

jørgen simonsen

An itinerant Dane and ESMOD honours graduate, whose dress Marisa Tomei wore when nominated for an
Academy Award in 2002, Jørgen Simonsen has been designing under his own name for several years, following
stints in houses with high glamour quotients such as Chanel, Valentino and Versace. What role do drawings
play in his work? 'A very important role,' he says. 'Centre stage.' The designer admits, 'I sometimes say that I am
computer-illiterate, jokingly', but 'more honestly, I believe that I can express *so* much more by my right hand, in
terms of having my artistic point of view come across, that all the technology in the world simply cannot compete!'

Opposite
'Ostrich feathered gala evening gown'
Pencil, colour crayons, pastel
and Pantone marker on paper,
Spring/Summer 2002

'Cocktail ensemble from the
Diana Vreeland collection'
Pencil, colour crayons, pastel
and Pantone marker on paper,
Autumn/Winter 2005–2006

'Evening gown from the
Diana Vreeland collection'
Pencil, colour crayons, pastel
and Pantone marker on paper,
Autumn/Winter 2005–2006

'Day skirtsuit from the centennial
anniversary of Georg Jensen'
Pencil, colour crayons, pastel
and Pantone marker on paper,
Spring/Summer 2003

'Late 30ties'
Fall 1939
Pastel on paper, 2005

'Coco between two styles and two worlds
1950 ... 1960'
Pastel on paper, 2005

'Early 60ties'
Pastel on paper, 2005

karl lagerfeld

'I never fall in love. I am just in love with my job,' Karl Lagerfeld, arguably the most prolific designer of his day, told *Interview* in 1975. That ardour is expressed not only in the profusion of his work, but also in his vibrant drawings. Born in Germany, Lagerfeld moved to Paris in his teens and started working as a designer-for-hire for labels such as Patou, Fendi and Chloé. He began designing for Chanel in 1983, and has his own line in addition.

Coco between two styles
and two worlds

1950 1960

2005

michael vollbracht

Michael Vollbracht, the Coty Award-winning designer, was born in Illinois and studied at Parsons School of Design in New York. His CV includes stints at Geoffrey Beene, Donald Brooks and Bill Blass. He also designed Bloomingdale's iconic Big Brown Bag. Vollbracht is equally well known as an illustrator: his work has appeared in *The New Yorker* and *The New York Times*. *Nothing Sacred*, a visual diary of his life in New York, was published in 1985. Surprisingly, Vollbracht's design process does not begin with a sketch. 'Fabric,' he states, 'always comes first in design; drawing second. Remember Chanel never sketched.'

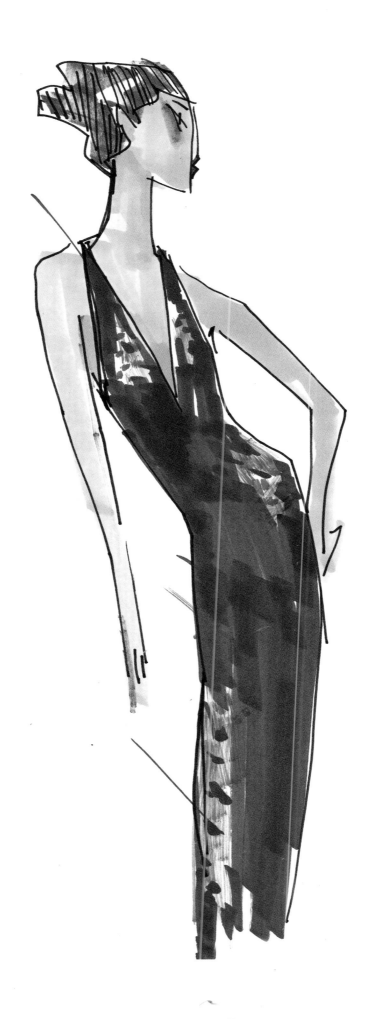

Mixed media on paper, 2004   Mixed media on paper, 1997

Mixed media on paper, 2005   Mixed media on paper, 2006

Untitled
Watercolours, coal and pencil on paper,
2006

'Little Wide Awake'
Watercolours, ink and pencil on paper,
2001

molly grad

'My thoughts are directly linked with a pencil,' says Molly Grad, a recipient of Colin Barnes and Nina De Yorke illustration awards. After completing her military service, Grad, an Israeli, enrolled at Central Saint Martins in London from which she earned Bachelor's and Master's degrees, both with distinction, and won the 2005 Chloé Award for Best Designer. Grad has worked with Stella McCartney and Yves Saint Laurent. 'Drawing plays a key role in my work,' she says. 'It is the starting position where all ideas come from, and the finishing point, when it is used as a detailed technical sketch, which is [in turn] used as a base to make a collection.'

'Agatha'
Ink on paper, 2005

Untitled
Watercolours and pencil on paper, 2006

Untitled
Watercolours and pencil on paper, 2006

Ink and coloured pencil on paper,
Fall 2007

Ink and coloured pencil on paper,
Fall 2007

peter som

'All my school notes had the margins filled with fashion sketches,' admits Peter Som, who was born in San Francisco. A graduate of Connecticut College and Parsons School of Design, Som launched his eponymous label in 2001 after gaining work experience at Bill Blass, Calvin Klein and Michael Kors. When designing, 'drawing is the first thing I do,' he explains. 'It's instinctive for me to pick up a pen and start drawing. I always dive right in. I never have the problem of staring at a blank piece of paper and not knowing what to draw. Once pen hits paper, I just let go.'

Pen and ink on paper, Spring 2007

SPRING
2007
PETER
SOM

PETER SOM
FOR
MANDY MOORE

Ink and coloured pencil on paper,
Spring 2007

'Peter Som for Mandy Moore
[Met Costume Ball 2006]'
Ink and coloured pencil on paper,
Spring 2006

'Fiesta: Carnaval'
Ink on paper, 2004

'Ten Piedad: Novicias'
Ink on paper, 2006

ramírez

'I have drawn since I was very little,' says Pablo Ramírez, the Argentine designer. 'I taught myself…. It was something very natural for me, like learning to walk or talk.' Ramírez, who is based in Buenos Aires and who studied at the university there, worked in the industry for several years before debuting his first collection in 2000. Called 'Casta', it was inspired by the nuns who had taught him as a child (he was the only boy in a class of 36 girls). 'It always pleases me to draw, and there are times,' the designer divulges, 'when I fantasize that I could try only to draw and not have to deal with all the rest of the things that are needed to make clothes….'

richard chai

People magazine might have named Richard Chai one of the sexiest men alive in 2004 – the year he launched his own line after creative directing at Marc Jacobs and TSE Cashmere – but the Korean-American Parsons grad doesn't go in for flash: he'd rather perfect a pattern that places a pocket in a pleat, or some such feat of technical construction. Who are his closest collaborators? His pencil-drawn 'girls'.

Opposite
Resort collection
Pencil on paper, 2008

Fall collection
Pencil on paper, 2007

rodarte

Kate and Laura Mulleavy, sisters two, are graduates of the University of California at Berkeley, where they studied art history and English literature respectively. 'When we were children,' Laura says, 'Kate would draw elaborate costumes and I would sign my name on them.' The sisters were born and still live at home in Pasadena and are self-taught illustrators and designers. How do their coveted confections come about? 'We sit together and sketch out ideas,' they say. 'All of our ideas come out through drawing and sketching. We do not do typical line drawings, but renderings of a feeling – a lightness – that we want to capture in our final product.'

Pencil on paper, 2007   Coloured pencil and ink on paper, 2007

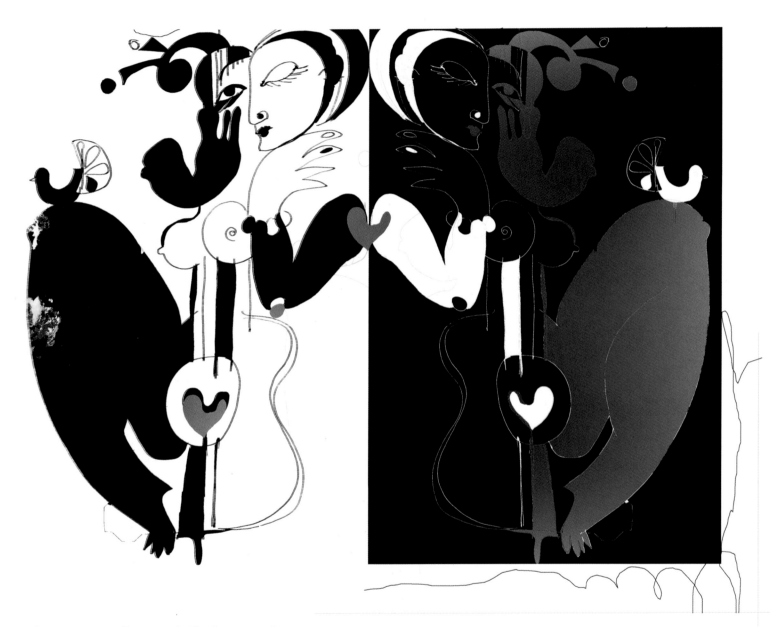

roksanda ilincic

'A final garment is a three-dimensional drawing,' says the London-based designer Roksanda Ilincic. 'I love observing this process – following the mood of the drawing being reshaped into a real garment, becoming alive and starting a different life.' Born in Belgrade, Ilincic studied Applied Arts and Design there and received her MA from Central Saint Martins in London. 'There are no restrictions of gravity or construction [when you draw],' she states. 'It's all about following initial ideas and intuition.'

Ink and collage on paper/computer finish,
Spring/Summer 2003

Invitation to collection
Ink and collage on paper/computer finish,
Spring/Summer 2005

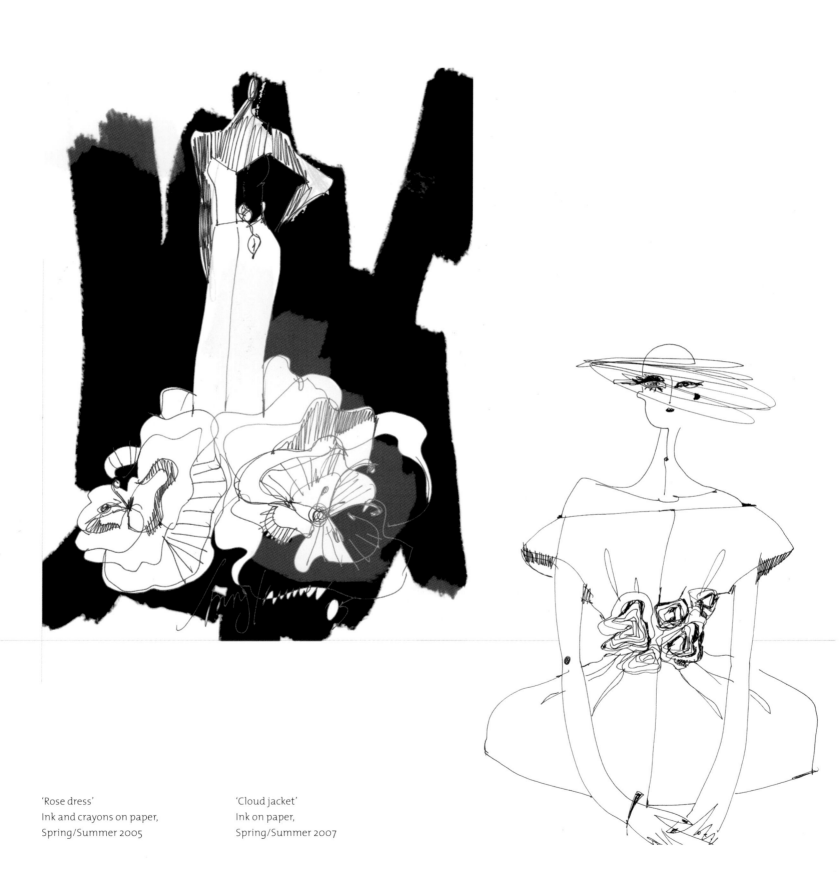

'Rose dress'
Ink and crayons on paper,
Spring/Summer 2005

'Cloud jacket'
Ink on paper,
Spring/Summer 2007

'Midnight dress'
Ink on paper,
Autumn/Winter 2005–2006

'Black tulip dress'
Ink on paper,
Autumn/Winter 2005–2006

Yellow + black intarsias + red Shoes

Sonia Rykiel

sonia rykiel

'I draw like I speak – naturally,' declares the 'Queen of Knits', Sonia Rykiel. A Parisian from her first breath
(she was also awarded a Légion d'Honneur in 1985), Rykiel makes sketches that reflect the Gallic insouciance
of her clothing. 'A drawing can convey many different unimaginable realities,' she says. 'There is a direct
and personal relationship with the artist's hand and medium. A drawing is open-ended, infinite and tactile.'

All images created specially for this publication
Ink on paper, 2007

stephen burrows

Born in Newark, New Jersey, Stephen Burrows started sewing at the age of eight because he wanted to make a present for his girlfriend. The son of an artist, this acclaimed designer – known for his use of jersey with a lettuce-edged finish – found that drawing came easily to him. He studied at the Philadelphia College of Art and the Fashion Institute of Technology. His design process begins with drawing – 'to capture the mood and posture of the collection I am about to do,' he explains. 'Then I go about trying to bring the sketch to life, literally.'

Mixed media on brown paper, 1989

Crayon on board, 1971

Ink on paper, 1973

'It's about content'
Watercolour and collage on paper,
2007

'Chevalier'
Watercolour on paper, 2007

CHEVALIER

susan cianciolo

Susan Cianciolo was once described as a 'darling of the New York fashion scene, the ragamuffin poster girl for creativity'. Born in Rhode Island, and a graduate of Parsons School of Design, Cianciolo is a master of multimedia disciplines: she paints, makes films, illustrates and designs. In 1995 Cianciolo launched a collection called RUN, featuring primitive-style garments with DIY elements that were often shown like installation art. 'It's everything to me to know what is next,' Cianciolo says. 'Drawing is abstract, and it explains to me what will be coming ahead and what story to tell and create. I trust it completely.'

'The Intervention'
Watercolour and collage on paper, 1983

Image created specially for this publication
Watercolour on paper, 2007

Both images
'Springtime'
Crayon and collage on paper, 2000

'The Thinker'
Pencil, ink, watercolour and tape on paper, 2001

terexov

'Since I left college, professional sketches have been my hobby,' says Alexander Terekhov, who studied drawing prior to enrolling at the Moscow Institute of Fashion, after which he interned at Yves Saint Laurent. 'This is something like yoga for me.' Nevertheless Terekhov notes that 'it is very common for the final product to have from 20 per cent to nothing of the original sketch'. As he explains, 'Once in process, you can realize that a different approach is required for a particular fabric. This is particularly true for creating dresses ... that do not distract one from the appearance of the owner, and yet have something special to [them].'

All images
Ink and watercolour on paper, 2003

All images
Ink and coloured pencils on paper,
Fall/Winter 2007

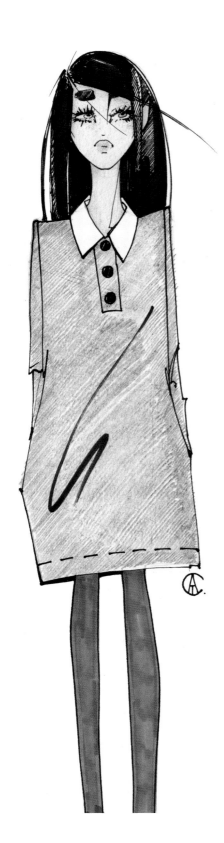

tibi

Amy Smilovic grew up amid a family of artists in Georgia, and herself studied life drawing. In 1997 she moved to Hong Kong, leaving a successful marketing career behind for fashion. Call it destiny. 'Drawing,' says Smilovic, who now runs a successful fashion business from SoHo in New York, 'is the first thing I do…' but it's not always easy. 'You can absolutely have days or weeks when you cannot draw a thing,' she admits. But 'when the mood hits and everything is on, I have to take advantage of it, no matter where I am – literally. I may even be at a movie or a restaurant and I have to grab a pen and paper. Those are the best times, when it is literally flowing out of you!'

Three images created specially for this publication
Pencil and ink on paper, 2007

Invitation to collection
Pencil and ink on paper, 2006, for Fall 2007

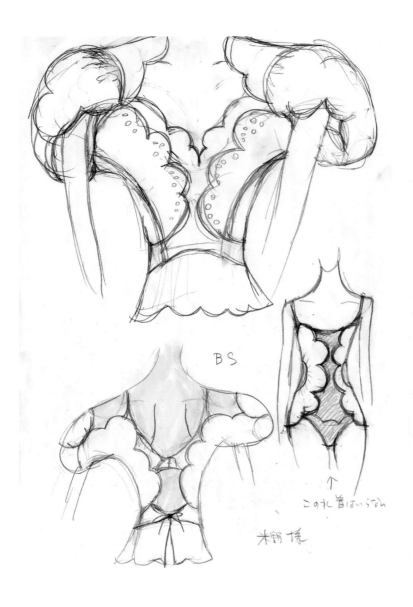

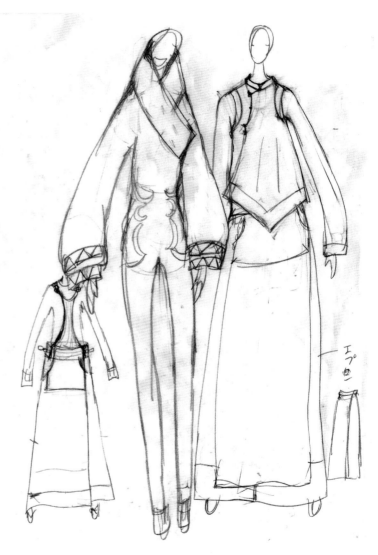

tsumori chisato

In 2006 Tsumori Chisato, an admirer of children's drawings and the work of Finnish artist Tove Jansson (of Moomin fame), released *Kawaii*, a collection of her artworks. Born in Tokyo, she studied at Bunka Fashion College before joining Issey Miyake in 1977 as head designer of Issey Sport. Thirteen years later Miyake helped Chisato launch her own line, for which she often designs unique prints. 'One of my childhood dreams,' she says, 'was to become a manga artist.'

Pencil and ink on paper, Spring 2007

Pencil and ink on paper, Autumn/Winter
2007–2008

TULEH—SP '05
ANTICIPATION
FOR: LIFE, LOVE, SEX, & FASHION...

Both images
'Anticipation'
Ink on vintage magazine pages,
2007, for Spring 2008

tuleh

Born in Appleton, Wisconsin, Bryan Bradley apprenticed at several prestigious New York fashion houses before launching Tuleh in 1998, inspired by Mary McCarthy's Vassar girl and all 'working girls who need to get dressed'. What the designer won't admit to is the origin of the name Tuleh, saying variously: 'I just thought it'd look good on a perfume bottle', or, 'It was a typo on the show invitation and we didn't notice until after they were mailed', or, 'I forgot'. That sense of humour is evident in Bradley's design process, from the notes he scrawls on his design sketches to the clothes themselves: 'a little twisted message; if someone wants to see it, it's there'.

CON
GRA
TUL
ATI
ONS

5 APRIL
2007
NYC

Image created specially for this publication
Ink on paper, April 2007

Ink on paper, Fall 2005

véronique leroy

'I am the most French of Belgian designers,' Véronique Leroy has said. Based in Paris, she was born in Liège. She enrolled at Studio Berçot in 1984, and worked with Didier Renard, Azzedine Alaïa and Martine Sitbon before setting up shop on her own in 1990. 'Femininity is my first ever preoccupation, and will still be my everlasting preoccupation in a collection,' she says. 'Both sexuality and femininity are present but it just depends on percentage.'

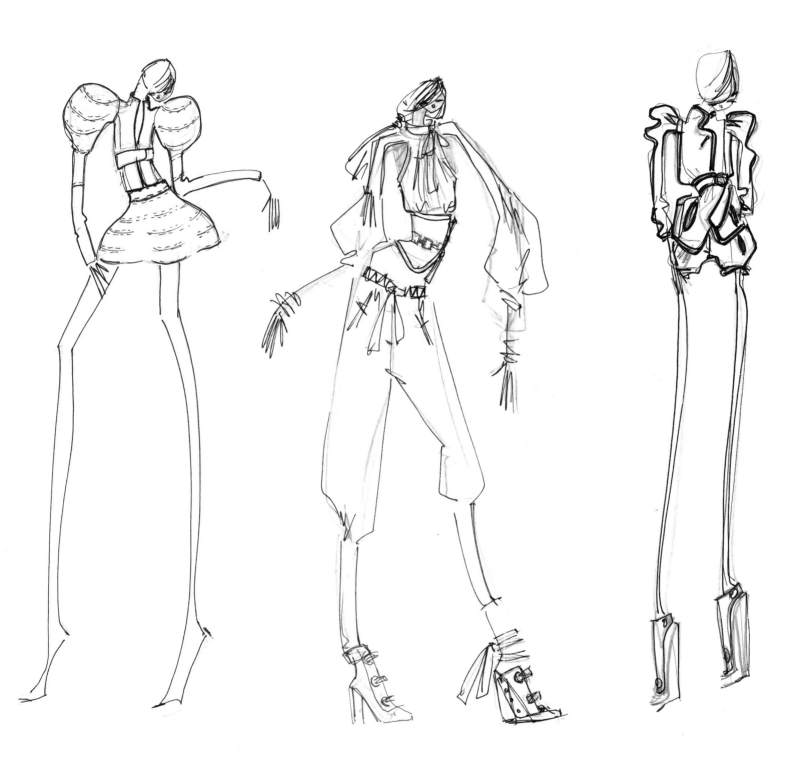

Ink on paper, Fall/Winter 2006–2007   Ink on paper, Spring/Summer 2005   Ink on paper, Spring/Summer 2007

'Revolution'
Ink and coloured pen on paper,
Winter 2001–2002

'Wonderland'
Ink and coloured pen on paper,
Winter 1996–1997

walter van beirendonck

'I enjoy every moment that I have the chance to draw and use my fantasy!' exclaims Brecht-born Walter Van
Beirendonck. In addition to designing his own line, Van Beirendonck heads the fashion department at the Royal
Academy of Antwerp, where he studied, and taught for many years. For his staff, Van Beirendonck executes
technical drawings; other drawings he does for himself, to decide 'on a total look'. 'I know that what I draw,' he
says, 'will have – once executed – the same impact and look as in my drawing. The sketches literally come alive.'

'Gender?'
Ink and coloured pen on paper,
Summer 2000

'Twinkle Twinkle Little Star'
Ink and coloured pen on paper,
Summer 1994

wunderkind by wolfgang joop

'My hand is the creative voice for the collection,' says Wolfgang Joop, who won his way into fashion. In 1970 the Potsdam-born designer and his then-wife took the top prizes in a magazine-sponsored contest. The designer began building the JOOP! label in 1981, only to sell his final stakes in the company in 2001 and establish Wunderkind three years later. He worked as a journalist/illustrator in Paris in the 1960s when it was forbidden to photograph or draw the collections in the salon, and remembers having to rush out of viewings and frantically sketch what he had seen. 'Drawing,' Joop says, 'is the most authentic, fast, communicative visual art that I master.'

To Caird
16.2.007

Wunderkind
Cashmeer
Dress
Fall/Winter
7/8

Pencil and ink on paper,
Fall/Winter 2007–2008

Ink and watercolour on paper,
Spring/Summer 2007

Ink and watercolour on paper,
with fabric swatches,
Fall/Winter 2007

y&kei water the earth

Gene Kang and Hanii Yoon are the Korean-born husband-and-wife team behind Y&Kei Water the Earth. Both studied fashion in San Francisco – Kang at the Academy of Art University and Yoon at the FIDM. While Yoon draws 'out of necessity', sketches flow from Kang's hand, and it is his work that is featured here. Every season the couple conducts intensive multimedia research on their collections, of which sketches are a big part, though they rarely hold onto them. 'We try to keep the ideas flowing by starting over. It's an Asian way of thinking, a Zen type of thinking,' Kang explains. 'It is our way to clear the mind to start anew.'

yoshikazu yamagata

'I always make a story which is like a picture book when I design something. That is kind of my original expression for fashion design,' admits Yoshikazu Yamagata, an award-winning Central Saint Martins grad who lives in Japan. 'I would like to work in a different style from existing designers' works,' Yamagata says. 'I guess it comes down to self-expression. The reason why I am interested in fashion is because of my desire to express myself. I never had confidence or star-like talents when I was small. For such a guy, fashion was something that made me able to express what I wanted to say in the most passionate and fun way.'

'A Long Story'
Ink on paper, Spring 2003

'The Weather Girl Collection'
Pencil and ink on paper, Winter 2002

All images
'The Weather Girl Collection'
Pencil and ink on paper, Winter 2002

'Homage to Braque',
Spring/Summer 1988

'Le Smoking', Fall/Winter 1966

'Toreador', Fall/Winter 1979

'Ballets russes'
Fall/Winter 1976–1977
(first sketch collection in colour)

yves saint laurent

In the 2002 documentary *Yves Saint Laurent: His Life and Times*, the legendary couturier reported: 'When I pick up
a pencil, I don't know what I'll draw. Nothing is planned. It's the miracle of the moment.... I start with a woman's face,
and suddenly the dress follows, or the garment takes shape.... It's a very pure form of creation, without any preparation,
without any vision.... And it is what impresses me most.... This surge of thought ... this capacity for creating clothes.
No one's more amazed than me. When the design's done, I'm very happy. Sometimes it works, sometimes not.
Then, you must stop drawing, go and do something else. But you will always come back to the paper and pencil.'

'Lady in orange frilled dress' from
Zandra Rhodes Handpainted
Collection
Pen, watercolour and gold pen
on paper, 2001

Lady in orange frilled dress.

Zandra Rhodes for Pologeorgis
Furs, published in *Pellice Moda
Fur World* magazine
Black pen and Pentel brush pen
on paper, *c.* 2003

*Zandra Rhodes
for
POLOGEORGIS FURS.

Yellow Mongolian lamb Chubby
with horizontal inserts of
Tie Dyed muskrat.*

zandra rhodes

As Suzy Menkes noted in a 2005 article in *The International Herald Tribune*, 'The essence of Zandra Rhodes is in her drawings and the technique of adapting them from paper images to three-dimensional clothes.' Drawing is a long-term obsession of the designer, who, as a student, not only drew every day, but brought her notebook to bed with her. These days Rhodes, a CBE and alumna of the Royal and the Medway Colleges of Art, finds the best time to draw is on vacation. Her continuing inspiration? 'Organic material and nature.'

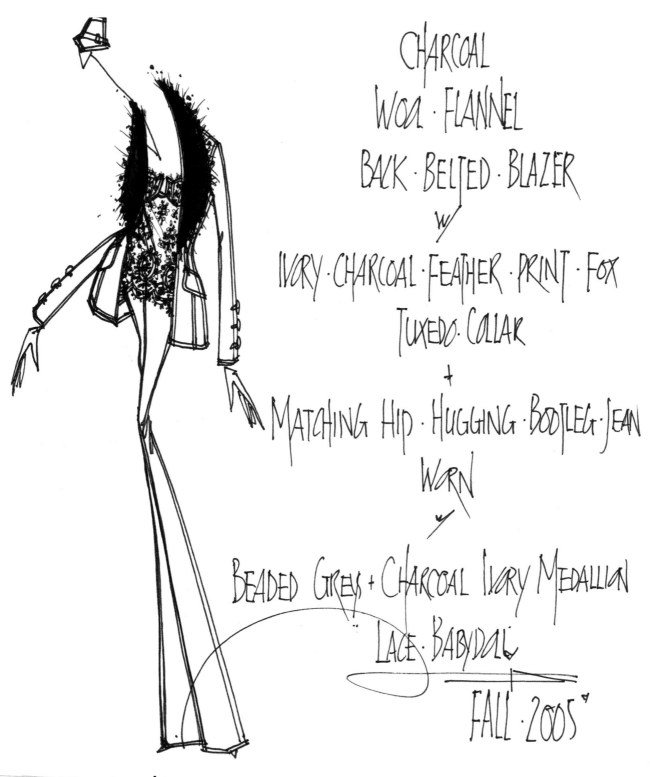

Ink on paper, Fall 2005

Ink on paper, Fall 2004

CHARCOAL
WOOL · FLANNEL
BACK · BELTED · BLAZER
w/
IVORY · CHARCOAL · FEATHER · PRINT · FOX
TUXEDO · COLLAR
+
MATCHING HIP · HUGGING · BOOTLEG · JEAN
WORN
↓
BEADED GREYS + CHARCOAL IVORY MEDALLION
LACE · BABYDOLL
FALL · 2005

zang toi

Years before he was knighted by the Sultan of Malaysia, in 1997, Zang Toi was 'sketching all over my poor parents' grocery store's counter top, floor, wall and account books'. Toi left home at eighteen and made his way through Toronto to New York, where he attended Parsons School of Design. He opened his own atelier in 1989. The designer – who sketches with a black roller pen on white paper – explains that a drawing is 'sketched over and over again until it's absolutely the way I envisioned or dreamt of a garment'. To Toi, the drawing is 'the very original vision of my design that retains [the] mysterious and magical process of my work'.

BLACK
ROYAL FOX + FEATHERS
QUEEN·BEES
WRAP
WORN
V
BLACK·COUTURE·SILK·DUCHESS
SATIN
BARONESS DE ROTHCHILD SKIRT
w/ BEADED TIGER + DRAGON
FALL · 2004

ROPES + ROPES
OF
DIAMOND
DRAPED
OVER
NAKE·BODICE

IVRY
SILK · VELVET
BLOUSE
w/
IVRY · LACE · ASCOT
WORN
w/
GREYS · BLUE · IVRY
ˇHOUSE OF T♡Iˇ
TARTAN
MINI · KILT
FALL · 2001

Both images
Ink on paper, Fall 2001

IVORY
SILK · VELVET
EVENING · SHIRT
+
IVORY · CHANTILLY · LACE ASCOT
WORN

GREYS · BLUE · IVORY
SATIN ORGANZA
♥ House of Toi ♥
TARTAN
KILTED
BALLSKIRT

FALL 2011

contacts

3.1 phillip lim
www.31philliplim.com

aitor throup
www.aitorthroup.com

alena akhmadullina
www.alenaakhmadullina.com

anna molinari
by rossella tarabini
www.annamolinari.it

antonio berardi
www.antonioberardi.com

antonio ciutto
www.antoniociutto.co.uk

badgley mischka
www.badgleymischka.com

bas kosters
www.baskosters.com

basso & brooke
www.bassoandbrooke.com

betsey johnson
www.betseyjohnson.com

boudicca
www.platform13.com

bruno frisoni
www.brunofrisoni.com
www.rogervivier.com

bruno pieters
www.brunopieters.com

burfitt
www.burfitt.com

chapurin
www.chapurin.com

Michael Vollbracht
Image created specially
for this publication
Pastel on paper, 2007

christian lacroix
www.christian-lacroix.fr

christian wijnants
www.christianwijnants.com

christopher kane
studiochristopherkane@googlemail.com

costello tagliapietra
www.jcrt.net

denis simachëv
www.denissimachev.com

doo.ri
www.doori-nyc.com

elise øverland
www.eliseoverland.com

gary graham
www.garyggraham.com

generra
by pina ferlisi
www.generra.com

giambattista valli
www.giambattistavalli.com

gianfranco ferré
www.gianfrancoferre.com

giles
info@mocommunications.com

gilles rosier
www.gillesrosier.fr

givenchy
by riccardo tisci
www.givenchy.com

gustavo arango
www.gustavoarango.com

hall ohara
www.hallohara.com

hanuk
www.hanuk.com

hervé l. leroux
www.hervelleroux.com

isaac mizrahi
www.isaacmizrahiny.com

james thomas
info@jamesthomas.com

jens laugesen
www.jenslaugesen.com

jørgen simonsen
By appointment only:
+33 6 72 08 75 23

karl lagerfeld
www.chanel.com
www.karllagerfeld.com

molly grad
info@mollygrad.com

peter som
www.petersom.com

ramírez
www.pabloramirez.com.ar

richard chai
www.rchai.com

rodarte
www.rodarte.net

roksanda ilincic
www.roksandailincic.com

sonia rykiel
www.soniarykiel.com

stephen burrows
www.stephenburrows.com

susan cianciolo
info@susancianciolo.com

terexov
www.terexov.com

tibi
www.tibi.com

tsumori chisato
www.a-net.com

tuleh
tulehnyc@aol.com

véronique leroy
www.veroniqueleroy.com

walter van beirendonck
www.waltervanbeirendonck.com

wunderkind
by wolfgang joop
www.wunderkind.de

y&kei water the earth
www.yandkei.com

yoshikazu yamagata
www.yoshikazuyamagata.jp

yves saint laurent
www.ysl.com

zandra rhodes
www.zandrarhodes.com

zang toi
zangtoi@houseoftoi.com

Contact details have been supplied
where available.

acknowledgments

I want to extend a thousand thanks to the people who helped bring this book into existence. *Merci bien* to the talented contributors and their in-house teams. They are: Phillip Lim and Erin Roberts; Aitor Throup; Alena Akhmadullina; Rossella Tarabini, Emanuela Barbieri, Flaminia d'Onofrio and Alessandra Marini at Blufin; Antonio Berardi and Luca Oroni; Antonio Ciutto; Mark Badgley, James Mischka and Rob Caldwell; Bas Kosters and Arthur Rambonnet; Bruno Basso and Christopher Brooke; Betsey Johnson and Agatha Szczepaniak; Brian Kirkby, Zowie Broach and Sarah Broach at Boudicca; Bruno Frisoni, Mariah Chase and Lidia Cerutti at Roger Vivier; Bruno Pieters and Karolien Van de Velde; Lovisa Burfitt and Kajsa Leanderson Laforge; Igor Chapurin, Alina Kovelenova and Anna Volokhova; Christian Lacroix and Bérangère Broman; Christian Wijnants; Christopher Kane and Tammy Kane; Jeffrey Costello, Robert Tagliapietra and Sammy; Denis Simachëv and Anna Dyulgerova; Doo-Ri Chung; Elise Øverland; Gary Graham; Pina Ferlisi and Sean Krebs; Giambattista Valli, Srdjan Prodanovic and Pauline; Giorgiana Magnolfi and Cristina De Rosas at Gianfranco Ferré; Giles Deacon; Gilles Rosier; Riccardo Tisci, Caroline Deroche Pasquier, Claus Estermann and Claire Vital at Givenchy; Gustavo Arango and Carolina Rodriguez; Yurika Ohara; Hanuk Kim; Hervé L. Leroux and Mariannick Vachat; Howard Tangye; Isaac Mizrahi, Korey Provencher and Jenny Lurie; James Thomas; Jens Laugesen and Victoria; Jørgen Simonsen; Karl Lagerfeld, Gretchen Gunlocke Fenton, Gerhard Steidl and Neil Palfreyman; Michael Vollbracht; Molly Grad; Peter Som, Marina and Hallie Chisman; Pablo Ramírez, Soledad and Staff Ramírez; Richard Chai; Kate and Laura Mulleavy and Mr Mulleavy at Rodarte; Roksanda Ilincic; Sonia Rykiel and Michelle Melton; Stephen Burrows and John Robert Miller; Susan Cianciolo, Danielle Kurtz and Sara Castro; Alexander Terekhov and Anna Grigorieva; Amy Smilovic and Liz Walker at Tibi; Tsumori Chisato; Bryan Bradley and Chellis Stoddard at Tuleh; Véronique Leroy and Jean-François Pinto; Walter Van Beirendonck; Wolfgang Joop, Marita Gottinger and Sarah-Jane Godman; Hanii Yoon and Gene Kang at Y&Kei Water the Earth; Yoshikazu Yamagata; Robin Fournier-Bergmann and Julien-Loïc Garin for Yves Saint Laurent at the Fondation Pierre Bergé (images © Fondation Pierre Bergé – Yves Saint Laurent; all rights reserved); Zandra Rhodes, Christiana and Jill McGregor; Zang Toi and Nana.

Molto grazie I say to my colleagues in publishing, fashion and public relations – experts whose help was invaluable. They are: Albert Kriemler, Eva Seiber and Silvia Bussert at Akris; Alexander Hertling at Totem PR; Alexandre Roux; Alexis Arnault at KCD; Alison Beckner at A-Net; Allison Sklaney; Ana Carolina Coelho at Bill Blass; Angelo Sensini at Angelo Sensini Communication; Anne Valerie Hash; Ava Scanlan at KPR; Bonnie Bien at La Presse; Bonnie Morrison at KCD; Brian Phillips at Black Frame; Caillianne, Samantha and Chloe Beckerman; Carrie Ellen Phillips at BPCM; Cathy Horyn; Cathy Sohn at Press Office; Cédric Edon at Karla Otto; Charlotte Niel at Suchel Presse; Christine Oh at BPCM; Christophe Decanin at Balmain; Clementine Chevalier at Zero Maria Cornejo; Coromoto Atencio; Courtney Kretchman at KPR; David Wilfert; Dee Salomon; Diesel ITS; Dirk Standen; Eugenia Rebolini; Farryn Weiner at Zac Posen; Fiona daRin; Giuliana Cohen Camerino; Greg Mills at Greg Mills PR; Hana Kim at Bill Blass; Hervé Pierre; Jason Wu; Jelka Music; John Huynh at AEFFE; Jonathan Green at KCD; Joy Jaffe; Judith Stora at Emanuel Ungaro; Katou Brandsma at Michele Montagne; Lindsay Thompson at Art & Commerce; Mandi Lennard at Mandi Lennard PR; Maria Cornejo; Maria Sgualdi at Guitar; Marie Le Cerf at Angelo Sensini Communication; Marie Moatti at BPCM; Matthew Williamson and Stephanie Wheatley; Mauricio Padhilla at MAO PR; Megan Salt at HL Group; The MisShapes; Molly Linden at KCD; Nicole Phelps; Nima Abbasi at Fly; Olivier Costa at BPCM; Peter Dundas; Prabal Gurung at Bill Blass; Roger Padhilla at MAO PR; Sarah Cristobal; Sebastien de Brito at Totem PR; Shoji Fuji; Steven Torres; Teppei; Tim Blanks; Trevor Tian at Black Frame.

Tack så mycket to my life-support team, who are: my husband, Carl Fredrik Persson, and my parents, and *muchas gracias* to Candy Pratts Price.

There would be no book without my colleagues at Thames & Hudson, the incomparable Jamie Camplin, Jenny Wilson, Karolina Prymaka and Helen Farr, to whom I extend a million thanks – and a virtual toast. Cheers!

Yoshikazu Yamagata
'The Naughty Boy Steals a Jacket from a Monster's House'
Pencil, ink and watercolour on singed paper, Spring 2004